WHERE WE MEET

WHERE WE MEET

A LENTEN STUDY OF SYSTEMS, STORIES, AND HOPE

Rachel Gilmore, Candace Lewis, Tyler Sit, and Matt Temple
of the Intersect Network

UPPER ROOM BOOKS®
NASHVILLE

ISBN: 978-0-8358-2048-6
Epub ISBN: 978-0-8358-2049-3

Cover design: Molly Mortimer, Minneapolis, MN
Interior design: PerfecType, Nashville, TN

Printed in the United States of America

Contents

Introduction

by Rachel Gilmore

When you look at the names on the cover of this book, you may find yourself asking, "Who are these people?" and "What is Intersect?"

Let's take the second question first. Intersect is a network of church innovators and spiritual entrepreneurs who seek to co-create communities that are postcolonial, equitable, contextual, diverse, and innovative.

The idea for Intersect emerged from an experience that each of us shared at one point or another. At some point, each of us was involved in planting a new faith community or church. When we looked around for resources, training, or mentors to guide us on this journey, we mostly found that the material available for church planting was dominated by a single demographic: older, white men. There's nothing inherently wrong with the perspective of older, white men, but it's only one perspective!

We also all faced some form of discrimination when attempting to get involved in the church planting community. I remember bringing my seven-month-old son to my first training event. I was still nursing and the nationally known trainer met me at the door and told me, "Women don't typically plant and young mothers never plant effectively so don't take it personally if this doesn't work out." Yeah, that happened.

It wasn't the only time. Later, I joined a cohort organized by one of the largest interdenominational church planting organizations and was listening as one of the keynote speakers announced that he was happy to see women in the room, but since he believed in the word of God, he didn't expect women to use anything that they learned to provide leadership to the church.

With all of these voices seeking to define me and shape me so early in my ministry, imagine my surprise when the Holy Spirit used my call to plant a church that grew from ten to more than 250—with another 200 online. Not only that, there is also a non-profit preschool connected to the church that serves the needs of the community. All that while raising my young son and having another child within the first year of launching.

After connecting with colleagues and friends that I respect in this field, we started Intersect: a Co-Planting Network in the fall of 2021. Our goal is to intentionally amplify and acknowledge powerful and important voices that have been ignored for way too long. That doesn't mean that we don't value the insights and contributions of our white, male friends; there are a lot of other people with a lot of important things to say! For instance, what does it mean to be acutely aware of the ways that the church has been a force of colonization, sexism and racism in our society? We want to create a space for shared influence and creating a shared vision for the future of the church.

The subtitle of this book is "A Lenten Study of Systems, Stories, and Hope." Already in this introduction you've heard a little bit about my story, in the reflections and devotions that make up this study you'll hear a little more. You'll also hear the stories of my colleagues, the other members of Intersect, as well as the stories of others who we think have something important to say.

In this introduction, you've also seen a glimpse of the systems that try to shape us, control us, and define us. These are the systems that have been left unchallenged and unquestioned for far too long, enhancing the privileges of those in power and pressing down the marginalized in our communities. We want to pull back the curtain and show these systems for what they are, the powers and principalities that are trying to tear down the kin-dom of God.

But you've also seen hope in this introductory story. You've seen that the Holy Spirit works to do great things in spite of the powers that be, in spite of the traumas of the past, and even in spite of our own failures. God can and will do things that are beyond our wildest imaginations.

The church is flawed. We are flawed. That's one of the things we're reminded of over and over again during Lent. We are reminded that from dust we came and to dust we shall return. There is pain, there is suffering, there is death, but there is also resurrection.

That's not just true for us, it's true for the church as well. You might be looking at the future of the church with fear or anxiety. You might even wonder if there will be a church. If there is, what will it look like? How will it change?

Over the next few weeks, we invite you to hear the good news! The future of the church is already here and it is bright and beautiful and diverse and divine!

In this devotional resource, we want to unpack this future with you, a future that is post-colonial, equitable, contextual, diverse, and innovative. We want to explore these core principles that have shaped our ministry work and that have also affected our personal spiritual lives. We think that they will be transformational for you and transformational for the church as well.

The first and last week of reflections in this study will be tied to the holy days of Ash Wednesday and Holy Week. In the first week, these reflections are designed to help prepare you for your journey; in the last week some friends of ours share their own stories from the journey as we head toward Easter Sunday.

Each of the other five weeks will cover one of our core principles of Intersect: post-colonial, equitable, contextual, diverse, and innovative. During each week, we'll look at this principle from a slightly different angle each day:

Sunday is a day to celebrate the resurrection of Christ, so we'll share a passage from Acts and explore how the early church lived out the message of the good news.

On Monday, we'll go back to the gospels to help us see these principles in the life and teachings of Christ.

Tuesdays will be dedicated to doing a systemic analysis where we examine the connections between our current culture and these themes and why the church may have drifted away from them.

Wednesday brings stories of hope, illustrating how these principles come to life and create the positive transformations within faith communities.

Thursdays are about being thirsty for change, as we explore the skill sets that you and your church can develop to live more deeply into these gospel truths.

Fridays are a time to wrestle with questions that don't have easy answers or might not have answers at all, as we continue this journey of self-awakening.

Finally, on Saturdays, we will turn to the practices that ground and guide us along the way. On this day, you will find a prayer practice or other activity that can help you absorb the message of the week.

As you embark on this journey, we pray that you are challenged and inspired. We pray that you are made uncomfortable in the best possible way. We pray that you learn something deep and meaningful about yourself, your community, your relationship with God, and the future of the church. We thank you for joining us during this season as we explore the vision and values that we believe will shape the future of the church.

Beginning the Journey

The journey you'll take through this book during Lent is an important one and like any important journey, it requires preparation. In the following devotionals, you'll hear from several different voices about the things we'll need to take with us as we explore systems of trauma. If we pack the right things before we go, we will find hope in these stories as well. With that in mind, we invite you to bring vulnerability, cultural humility, curiosity, grace, repentance, and forgiveness with you as you embark on this trip with us.

Ash Wednesday

by Matt Temple

Reading

2 Corinthians 12:8-10

Three times I appealed to the Lord about this, that it would leave me, but he said to me, "My grace is sufficient for you, for power is made perfect in weakness." So I will boast all the more gladly of my weaknesses, so that the power of Christ may dwell in me. Therefore I am content with weaknesses, insults, hardships, persecutions, and calamities for the sake of Christ, for whenever I am weak, then I am strong.

Reflection

Do you remember the first time you felt weak or vulnerable—the moment you realized that the world could be a perilous place, with that realization looming over you like a constant threat? For me, it's challenging to pinpoint when that awareness set in. Perhaps my parents' divorce when I was just two years old played a significant role, but I can't recall a time when the world didn't feel threatening to me. I do remember, at a very young age, seeing photos of my mom's new family enjoying themselves at Disney World, but I was conspicuously absent from those pictures. The same held true for my dad and his new family. Raised as an only child among five brothers and two sisters, I've long grappled with the question, "Where do I belong?" Having a clear sense of belonging and a place to call home helps us internalize security and feel safe in the world. It's not that the world becomes entirely safe for us; rather, we have a refuge to retreat to when the storms come. Growing up without a clear sense of home, without that refuge, makes the quest to find one's place in the world daunting.

In early childhood, there is a developmental process called "proximity seeking and secure base." In a healthy environment, this is the process we go through when we explore the world around us and learn to feel safe within that world. Think of toddlers visiting a public park for the first time. Their guardian represents safety, but as they look out and see all the other children laughing and having fun, they are filled with a desire to explore. At first, children cling tightly to their guardians, but gradually they let go and venture out. If they start to feel unsafe, they can return to their secure base to reassure themselves. In a nurturing environment, this process eventually leads to the child internalizing a secure base and finding the courage to explore. However, in an unhealthy environment, a child is compelled to venture out, but is filled with anxiety and fear, with nowhere to go for safety. Along the way, that child will seek things to place trust in, things that give a sense of security in the world. The child becomes adept at hiding vulnerability and insecurity, often discovering gifts and strengths to hide behind, pretending that everything is alright.

As I reflect on my own spiritual journey, I've realized that, for me, religion was a secure base, but it was also the place where I hid, pretending that everything was okay. Dogmatic religious beliefs offered simple answers to the complexities of a world that I couldn't control. Religion provided a clear road map for appeasing God and finding success in life. Finally, for someone who always felt vulnerable and inferior, religion gave me clear rules to follow, rules I believed would help me ultimately win and make me appear superior. It was a façade that gave me the illusion of safety. It was a façade that gave me the illusion of strength.

In our world, we spend a tremendous amount of energy to conceal our weaknesses, to pretend to be something we're not, and to avoid showing the vulnerability and insecurity we truly feel. We're told to be strong. And then, along comes this beautiful holy day we call Ash Wednesday, a day that gives us permission to be weak, to acknowledge our limitations, and to repent. This journey of repentance is no easy task. It requires us to unlearn our misconceptions about what strength looks like and confront the idols we've looked to for salvation. It forces us to interrogate the illusions we've created about safety, success, and simple answers.

Repentance compels us to confront our own weaknesses and the lies we've told ourselves and the world. It demands that we acknowledge the ways in which we've fallen short, both as individuals and as a collective. Self-reflection is not easy. We must look into the eyes of that scared little child living inside of us and say, "It is okay to be scared. You are loved and accepted just the way you are." When we embrace our vulnerability and allow God's grace to enter our lives, we reveal a strength and resilience that is true and genuine.

As we embark on this journey together, my prayer for each of us is that we will embrace the spirit of Ash Wednesday. When the light shines on our vulnerabilities, instead of rushing back to our secure base of religious dogma, may we find grace in repentance and vulnerability, discovering a holier internal secure base.

Questions

- Have you ever used religion or any belief system as a way to hide your vulnerabilities or fears? How did it affect your life?

- How do you typically cope with feelings of weakness or insecurity? Do you feel pressure to appear strong, even when you don't feel that way?

- What aspects of your life would you like to acknowledge, repent, or seek grace for? How might embracing vulnerability and authenticity lead to a holier and more secure sense of self?

Thursday

by Matt Temple

Reading

Matthew 5:8

"Blessed are the pure in heart, for they will see God."

Luke 10:29-37

But wanting to vindicate himself, he asked Jesus, "And who is my neighbor?" Jesus replied, "A man was going down from Jerusalem to Jericho and fell into the hands of robbers, who stripped him, beat him, and took off, leaving him half dead. Now by chance a priest was going down that road, and when he saw him he passed by on the other side. So likewise a Levite, when he came to the place and saw him, passed by on the other side. But a Samaritan while traveling came upon him, and when he saw him he was moved with compassion. He went to him and bandaged his wounds, treating them with oil and wine. Then he put him on his own animal, brought him to an inn, and took care of him. The next day he took out two denarii, gave them to the innkeeper, and said, 'Take care of him, and when I come back I will repay you whatever more you spend.' Which of these three, do you think, was a neighbor to the man who fell into the hands of the robbers?" He said, "The one who showed him mercy." Jesus said to him, "Go and do likewise."

Reflection

When I was around ten years old, I woke up as normal on one particularly blustery day, only to look out my bedroom window and discover a blanket of white crystals covering the ground. Thus, the greatest ritual of midwestern childhood began.

I raced down the stairs, poured myself a bowl of Fruity O's (because we shopped at Aldi, naturally), and turned on the radio, waiting expectantly for official word that our school day was canceled. My mom urged me to get ready just in case, but I had faith! The moment our school's name was announced, our dining room filled with palpable joy. The snow had gifted us with the ultimate midwestern treasure: a snow day. And we all knew exactly how to celebrate—we were going sledding.

Bundled up in layers, my brothers and I loaded our gear and our sleds into our large conversion van, and my mom drove us to the grade school about a mile away. This school had an epic sledding hill, consisting of three thrilling sections. It started steep at the top, then leveled off for a bit. With enough momentum, you could make it through the flat section and hit the second hill. Beyond the second hill, the ground leveled out again before plummeting into a third and final descent. No one worried about the third hill though because no one ever got enough speed to make it there. That was for the best though because the large brick wall of the school sat at the bottom of the third hill. You may already see where this story is going.

On this particular day, my sled raced down faster than ever! I effortlessly made it to the third hill, but as the school building came closer and closer, I froze. The next thing I knew, I was in the hospital with twenty stitches in my chin, a nice bruise on my face, and a mild concussion.

In our brains, just above the brainstem, there's a region called the limbic system. It's one of the older parts of our brain and it's responsible for the fight, flight, and freeze responses, that have ensured humanity's survival for thousands and thousands of years. Our limbic system takes in external information, processes it in an instant, and gives us a nudge to do whatever is necessary to survive at that moment, like bailing off a sled. Interestingly, something like the limbic system is present in nearly every mammal on earth, so it's not uniquely human.

What sets us apart as humans is the prefrontal cortex, the youngest part of our brain. Among its many functions, it grants us the capacity for self-reflection. Unlike the limbic system, using the prefrontal cortex doesn't come naturally to us. This can lead to situations where these two systems come into conflict. Our limbic system may see something new or different as a threat, while our prefrontal cortex enables us to look within, challenge our assumptions, and even question our beliefs.

This is why I've come to love the sixth beatitude. It reminds us of our capacity for introspection. It invites us to consider that the biggest barrier to seeing God might not be some external, ideological threats, but something internal that requires honest and humble investigation.

As we embark on this Lenten journey, one essential tool we need is cultural humility. At the most basic level, cultural humility is the recognition that context matters. Each of us has been uniquely shaped by our contexts and our life experiences, leading to differences among us. Acknowledging these differences is an important step, but it is only a first step. We must then layer on faith, hope, and love so that we no longer see differences as threats but as invitations to grow in understanding and empathy.

Cultural humility is a concept that emphasizes self-reflection, openness, and a willingness to engage with diverse cultures and perspectives. It recognizes our limited cultural knowledge and underscores the importance of approaching others with respect, curiosity, and a genuine desire to understand their unique experiences.

Questions

- How do I approach encounters with people from different cultural backgrounds? Do I approach them with an open mind and a willingness to learn, or do I hold on to preconceived notions or biases?

- How do I respond when confronted with my own cultural blind spots or biases? Am I defensive and unwilling to engage in self-reflection, or am I open to acknowledging and addressing these areas of growth?

- How do I respond to moments of cultural misunderstandings or conflicts? Do I approach these situations with patience, curiosity, and a willingness to learn, or do I become defensive or quick to judge?

Friday

by Jasper Peters

Jasper Peters (he/him) is a church planter and the lead pastor of Belong Church in Denver, Colorado.

Reading

John 17:20-24

I ask not only on behalf of these, but also on behalf of those who will believe in me through their word, that they may all be one. As you, Father, are in me and I am in you, may they also be in us, so that the world may believe that you have sent me. The glory that you have given me I have given them, so that they may be one, as we are one, I in them and you in me, that they may become completely one, so that the world may know that you have sent me and have loved them even as you have loved me. Father, I desire that those also, whom you have given me, may be with me where I am, to see my glory, which you have given me because you loved me before the foundation of the world.

Reflection

From my earliest memories, I looked up to my cousin. He carries himself with self-respect while extending kindness, respect, and abundance to everyone he meets. When I was younger, I remember thinking that I wanted to be like him when I grew up. I felt so mature when he would offer me the dignity of asking for my advice or opinion.

There are a number of things that separate my cousin and me, both physically and ideologically. We have always lived far apart—he in Atlanta with his family; I in Denver with mine. It's only in adulthood that we've had the chance to build a closer relationship. A few years ago, he reached out and asked if we could talk on the phone. He had questions for me, a former Baptist turned Methodist pastor, regarding my interpretation of scripture and understanding of human sexuality. Initially, I was nervous, fearing that our conversation might mirror some of the toxic exchanges often found online. Instead, we approached each other with a sense of holy curiosity. We questioned the scriptures together, each sharing our understanding and weighing our insights against our personal experiences.

We did not agree that day, yet upon reflection, the sharpest points of disagreement escape me. What I recall is much more important: we began and ended our conversation with curiosity and grace. He started with questions, I provided responses, and he accepted them without trying to counter. We allowed space open for contemplation, a blessed holy silence, providing room for processing and reflection.

I love my cousin, and I know that he loves me. I didn't have to worry about him trying to prove me wrong, trying to score points through digs on social media, or rushing me for an immediate answer. Love, grace, and respect formed the foundation of our conversation and our relationship.

We spoke for several hours that day. We ended by encouraging each other to continue being thoughtful and to continue extending grace; then we prayed for each other. We continue to talk, both of us driven not by the need to be understood, but by a desire to understand. Whenever I think about my cousin and our talks, I wish that the church could embody what we share. We don't pretend to agree, nor do we strive for politeness. Instead, we choose truth, love, and grace. We also talk about other things in our lives. We talk about what we think Jesus might lament most about society, or the last time he was able to see my mother, and the way the world fails to understand our children and their unique needs. We talk about the things that make us human, that make us Christian, that make us family, the things that make us one.

This, I believe, is what Jesus intended for the church to be and continues to desire today. This kind of curiosity and openness is precious, it is earned over time. While the church often falls short in modeling this curiosity, perhaps it can be rekindled and nurtured one person and one conversation at a time. It can be hard to place our trust in the church relearning how to love and trust. But, if there is reconciliation to be sought, love to be fostered, and grace to be extended before we seek to receive it, let it be done like this—one person to another.

Questions

- When you speak with someone who has different views from yours, do you approach the conversation with grace, love, and a curiosity to understand?

- Do you open yourself up to friendships or relationships with those who think differently from you, or do you surround yourself with voices like your own?

Saturday

by Rachel Gilmore

Reading

James 5:16

Therefore confess your sins to one another, and pray for one another, so that you may be healed. The prayer of the righteous is powerful and effective.

Ephesians 4:31-32

Put away from you all bitterness and wrath and anger and wrangling and slander, together with all malice. Be kind to one another, tender-hearted, forgiving one another, as God in Christ has forgiven you.

Reflection

My first job after college was at a local preschool in Dayton, Ohio. Each class had one or two kids who struggled with kindness, and they resorted to pushing, hitting, or throwing things at their classmates. I'll never forget the first time the head teacher, Jodi, took one of these children aside to help him understand the consequences of his actions. The child defiantly yelled back, "I told them I was sorry! Leave me alone, I said I was sorry."

Jodi responded "No, we don't just say 'I'm sorry,' we also ask, 'How can I make it better?'" Those words struck me profoundly. They reminded me of the Hebrew word for repentance, *shuv*, which means to make a 180-degree turn and head in the opposite direction. Repentance cannot be hollow words that offer no hope of true change. Repentance must be accompanied by action and a commitment to change course and do things differently.

As you engage with this book over the next several weeks, you may have days where you feel the need to apologize to God, to others, and to yourself. When you seek repentance for the conscious and unconscious harm you've done to the kin-dom of God, when you grasp the consequences of the systemic racism and discrimination around you and ask for forgiveness, please don't do so with empty words. Take the time to really think about the changes, both in thoughts and actions, that you must embrace to truly repent and move in a better direction.

A vital part of forgiveness is confession—to God, to others, and to yourself. While confession can be intimidating and make us vulnerable, it can also be life-giving. When I'm confessing my failures to others, I try to stick to one fundamental rule: avoid using the word "but." Phrases like, "I'm sorry I hurt you, *but* I was tired," or, "I'm sorry I said that, *but* I didn't know better," undermine confession. "But" attempts to justify or defend our actions and is unhelpful in the moment of confession. Perhaps there is a place for it later, in deeper discussions, but leave it out of your initial confession.

Finally, seeking forgiveness—whether from God, from others, or from ourselves—can be a challenging process. Forgiveness is not static; it's a dynamic journey. It involves discovering what forgiveness looks like and what it means for the future of the relationship. There are times when I have forgiven people, even when they haven't sought forgiveness, as a path to liberate myself and move from the posture of a victim to that of a survivor.

Forgiveness can mean different things in different situations. Sometimes it means restoring a relationship, while other times, forgiveness means letting go of the wrong while keeping your distance and maintaining safe and healthy boundaries. But what if you're not ready to forgive? What if the racism, discrimination, or evil you've endured feels too raw and traumatic to begin the process of forgiveness?

Consider my twin sister's experience in Rwanda, where she worked with Hutu and Tutsi people after the genocide. During the ten months she lived there, she worked on her dissertation, which was focused on how to decrease levels of unforgiveness. When I asked why she emphasized reducing unforgiveness rather than just teaching about forgiveness directly, she explained that some of the people had endured so much pain that they were not able to start with forgiveness. Instead, by spending time empathizing with their enemies and understanding their perspective, they could gradually decrease their unforgiveness, hopefully opening the door to forgiveness.

One example she shared was the story of a woman we'll call "Kayitesi." Kayitesi's mother was murdered by a man who refused to confess to the crimes he had committed. Shortly before this man was to be released from prison, Kayitesi told my sister, "There are two types of people, those who ask for forgiveness and those who do not. Remember that. Those who confess, who actually feel sorry for what they did, are the ones you can forgive. Those that do not feel bad, do not want forgiveness and you cannot forgive."

I share this with you to encourage you. If the thought of forgiveness feels wrong at this moment or too painful, I invite you to invest your time and energy in trying to see things from the viewpoint of others. Perhaps, in time, forgiveness will feel like a safer option to you as we move forward on this journey together.

Questions

- Is there something you need to confess and repent (to God, to others, to yourself)? If so, find a way to name and release that sin.

- Think about a way that you have done harm or wronged someone (either in the past or in an ongoing situation). How can you make it better? What would the *shuv* process look like for you?

- As you ponder the act of forgiveness, do a heart check to determine if you are ready to seek or receive forgiveness. What might forgiveness look like when it comes to addressing some of the larger issues of colonization, discrimination, and racism in our society and in our churches?

Diversity

As I travel the country, church folks often ask me, "How do we get young people in the church?" Sometimes they ask with a furrowed brow of determination, and sometimes they ask with a fearful tremble of the lip. If I'm in a white church, they tend to follow up with, "Our church is so white. How do we get a worship leader of color?"

In many ways, I empathize with these questions. My antennae is always up, always asking, "Who isn't in the room?" But in many of these communities, the thing that's missing is a realistic understanding of what is required for true diversity. As a church planter who has led a multiracial community for almost a decade, I still have regular conversations with my leaders about how we need to stretch ourselves to reach for more diversity. This week's devotions explore what God says about the exercise of diverse community building, and how we can move closer to solidarity and God-breathed justice.

Sunday

Reading

Acts 8:26-40 (CEB)

An angel from the Lord spoke to Philip, "At noon, take the road that leads from Jerusalem to Gaza." (This is a desert road.) So he did. Meanwhile, an Ethiopian man was on his way home from Jerusalem, where he had come to worship. He was a eunuch and an official responsible for the entire treasury of Candace. (Candace is the title given to the Ethiopian queen.) He was reading the prophet Isaiah while sitting in his carriage. The Spirit told Philip, "Approach this carriage and stay with it."

Running up to the carriage, Philip heard the man reading the prophet Isaiah. He asked, "Do you really understand what you are reading?"

The man replied, "Without someone to guide me, how could I?" Then he invited Philip to climb up and sit with him. This was the passage of scripture he was reading:

> Like a sheep he was led to the slaughter
>   and like a lamb before its shearer is silent
>   so he didn't open his mouth.
> In his humiliation justice was taken away from him.
>   Who can tell the story of his descendants
>   because his life was taken from the earth?

The eunuch asked Philip, "Tell me, about whom does the prophet say this? Is he talking about himself or someone else?" Starting with that passage, Philip proclaimed the good news about Jesus to him. As they went down the road, they came to some water.

The eunuch said, "Look! Water! What would keep me from being baptized?" He ordered that the carriage halt. Both Philip and the eunuch went down to the water, where Philip baptized him. When they came up out of the water, the Lord's Spirit suddenly took Philip away.

The eunuch never saw him again but went on his way rejoicing. Philip found himself in Azotus. He traveled through that area, preaching the good news in all the cities until he reached Caesarea.

Reflection

As a warm-up for this week of reflections, think for a moment and write down three reasons diversity should be important to the church. Take a few minutes now and list the reasons here:

1.

2.

3.

During his ministry, Jesus formed a community with people who were diverse in economic standing, ethnic group, gender, ability, age, and more. His ministry marked the dawn of a multinational, multiracial movement. Why is this significant?

Perhaps the story of Philip and the eunuch can shed some light on this matter. In the cultural context of that time, eunuchs were considered neither fully male nor female; they occupied a distinct gender category. Additionally, the "Ethiopia" mentioned here, though still in Africa, is not identical to the modern geopolitical region of the same name. Consider those two pieces of information and then think about how remarkable it is that early in the book of Acts, early in the history of the church, Philip baptizes and commissions a foreigner—someone with darker skin and a gender-minority status. Take a moment to think about how radical that is!

More importantly, this wasn't just a clever idea Philip had. He was guided by the Spirit. This was a divine mandate. This teaches us that diversity is not just a preference; it's a divine imperative.

Diversity isn't merely a concept; it drives discipleship. When we cultivate diverse community, we become more complete individuals because we discover our kinship with people who are different from us.

Furthermore, diversity is a challenge to the empire. It is a challenge to the structures of power and oppression that Jesus aimed to dismantle. These structures thrive on favoritism, with a consolidated privileged group exploiting a defined underclass to maintain their power and provide comfort for the privileged. When we foster diverse communities, we dispel the myth that there is one right way of doing things, and we amplify voices that the empire has long silenced.

I could keep going, but I think the message is clear. This week, we'll explore the creation of diverse communities, even the less glamorous aspects. I urge you to approach this week with unwavering conviction that diversity is not just something we should do out of guilt or obligation. Embrace diversity with the same fervor the Spirit imbued in Philip. The idea that we "should" be diverse will not get us far. But a love for diversity and a passion for all it demands will.

Questions

- Why is diversity in our faith communities and movements worth it?

- What is God telling you about diverse community?

Reading

Luke 22:14-20 (CEB)

When the time came, Jesus took his place at the table, and the apostles joined him. He said to them, "I have earnestly desired to eat this Passover with you before I suffer. I tell you, I won't eat it until it is fulfilled in God's kingdom." After taking a cup and giving thanks, he said, "Take this and share it among yourselves. I tell you that from now on I won't drink from the fruit of the vine until God's kingdom has come." After taking the bread and giving thanks, he broke it and gave it to them, saying, "This is my body, which is given for you. Do this in remembrance of me." In the same way, he took the cup after the meal and said, "This cup is the new covenant by my blood, which is poured out for you.

Reflection

I recognize that discussing the Last Supper this early in Lent may seem out of liturgical order, but it's the perfect story to contemplate when reflecting on the creation of a diverse community.

Consider what this event looked like from an outside, and slightly cynical, perspective. From that angle, Jesus' farewell dinner was an absolute and unmitigated mess. Peter is spiraling out and asking who gets to sit at Jesus' right hand in heaven. Half the group apparently hadn't been listening for the past two years and completely missed the memo that Jesus was imminently going to die. Judas literally sold out, yet no one seems to be holding him accountable. Random people are crying, and to top it off, they had forgotten to make dinner reservations and had to borrow someone else's space!

This is not an entirely scholarly read of the Last Supper, but as a church leader, there's a subtle satisfaction in this image. Jesus succeeded in bringing together a diverse group, but it didn't mean everything was hunky-dory. Following Jesus didn't magically stop the disciples from being human and being flawed. Seen this way, the Last Supper can be a source of comfort for those whose communities don't quite feel like something out of a Hallmark movie.

After all, the ultimate goal isn't to create a rigid army where diverse people unquestioningly follow orders. The goal is for people to experience genuine freedom and for a diverse group of individuals to choose community together. If that's the goal, the only path to community growth is through co-creation, working collaboratively rather than in a didactic manner.

All of this ties into our relationship with control. Control makes things nice and tidy. My socks, for example, are impeccably folded and organized because I have full control over the space. I get a little boost each morning when I open my drawer and see that things are exactly how I want them to be. Communities, however, aren't as orderly as sock drawers. Co-creation demands letting go of some control and trusting people who see things differently from you.

This means that, sometimes to my chagrin, my church space is messier—both literally and figuratively—than my sock drawer. Despite shared covenants, intentional onboarding, and a community-created style guide, many things fall into the "that's-not-how-I-would-have-done-it" category.

A vital skill for disciples is distinguishing between what must be held firmly for the sake of the gospel and what must be held loosely for the sake of community. This is especially true for leaders. In this context, perhaps the Last Supper unfolded exactly as God intended, and it serves as a model for us as we strive to grow as followers of Jesus.

Questions

- What thoughts arose for you as you considered that the Last Supper was messy?

- When have you co-created something and seen it turn out well? What did you learn from that experience?

- Is it harder for you to relinquish control or to self-advocate? How do you think God speaks to that?

Reading

Acts 10:9-16 (CEB)

At noon on the following day, as their journey brought them close to the city, Peter went up on the roof to pray. He became hungry and wanted to eat. While others were preparing the meal, he had a visionary experience. He saw heaven opened up and something like a large linen sheet being lowered to the earth by its four corners. Inside the sheet were all kinds of four-legged animals, reptiles, and wild birds. A voice told him, "Get up, Peter! Kill and eat!"

Peter exclaimed, "Absolutely not, Lord! I have never eaten anything impure or unclean."

The voice spoke a second time, "Never consider unclean what God has made pure." This happened three times, then the object was suddenly pulled back into heaven.

Reflection

When you inquire about dinner recommendations in Minneapolis, most people will light up and say, "Owamni!" Then, quickly, their eyes will dim as they apologetically say, "But you would have needed to get your reservation six weeks ago." Regardless of the time of year, securing a table at Owamni demands careful planning well in advance.

Owamni, the brainchild of The Sioux Chef, Sean Sherman, a member of the Oglala Lakota nation, born in Pine Ridge, South Dakota, stands as a beacon of culinary ingenuity. Internationally acclaimed for his commitment to revitalizing indigenous food systems, Sherman's restaurant exclusively features ingredients available pre-colonization—no sugar, no dairy, no wheat flour.

Depending on the season, even crickets are on the menu. Many cultures have long embraced insects as a sustainable source of protein, but this presented me with an unexpected moral dilemma. I had been a vegetarian for a decade, and I had been pretty strict about it. I used to be the person cautiously inquiring, "Is there chicken broth in this soup?" But eating at Owamni that evening with my boyfriend challenged me to ask a new question: "Does eating crickets count as eating meat?"

While my vegetarianism is a personal choice, Peter's dietary guidelines were woven into the fabric of his faith. These practices were deeply ingrained and passed down through generations of the Judeo-Christian tradition. Peter would have had carefully-honed instincts about what was acceptable to eat and what wasn't after years of parents and community members pointing at animals and saying, "We don't eat that—not you, not our family, not anyone who is Jewish." Then, in a twist of fate, God (who was the source of these food restrictions in the first place) presented Peter with a vision, offering a feast of unclean animals and inviting Peter to eat.

I love that Peter's instinctual response is, "Absolutely not, Lord!" He couldn't catch himself after all those years of training about what was clean or unclean. It was the reaction of someone confronted with a foreign and unsettling notion, something like disgust. But God's message transcended mere dietary advice. Shortly after this vision, Peter had an encounter with Gentiles that shattered his preconceptions of who was relevant to his faith community. In Acts 10:45-47, we read that the Gentiles received the Holy Spirit and Peter realized that God's love extended beyond ethnic boundaries.

Most sermons about this passage focus on a pretty straightforward message. They highlight Peter's transformation and God's love for all people, not just those who are like us. Like Peter, we are called to share this love with people who are different from us, even people we find disgusting.

But this interpretation falls short. As a member of the queer community, I have been called disgusting. I have been ridiculed as vile, sinful, and dangerous. As a result, I am suspicious of interpretations that conclude that this is a story about "us" mustering the courage to reach out to "the unwanted."

This chapter in Acts isn't about Peter; it's about the Gentiles, particularly one leader named Cornelius. Cornelius, who was not Jewish, gave generously to those who needed it and prayed to God constantly. Cornelius revolutionizes the way Peter and his community relate to people outside their group.

In many church-based diversity initiatives, especially in predominantly white churches, the emphasis often centers on someone from the majority group showing courage in engaging with someone from the minority group. This is a Peter-centered lens instead of a Cornelius-centered one. Diversity is portrayed as, "Look at us opening our doors to diversity by hiring a certain worship leader or renting one unused classroom to a nonprofit!" Instead, it should be, "Look at the amazing work God is doing outside our church; what an honor to consider ourselves part of it."

Returning to Owamni, my long-standing vegetarianism had conditioned me to be disgusted by meat-based food. Initially, as I savored expertly prepared crickets, a hint of ego crept in, thinking, "Look at how cultured and brave I am." However, as I looked around and considered The Sioux Chef's remarkable accomplishments in creating this restaurant and reimagining colonized food systems, I realized that the focal point wasn't my palate but rather The Sioux Chef's transformative work. This wasn't a gimmick; it was the continuation of a legacy that existed before me and will endure without me. It was my honor to be a part of it.

And, I'll be real; the crickets were also delicious.

Questions

- Consider an event involving injustice that is relevant to your community. How would that same story be told differently when centering the well-intentioned privileged versus centering the marginalized?

- No one person embodies all marginalized identities. Who is someone in your life you could get behind, not out of charity but out of a desire to participate in a larger movement of God?

Wednesday

Reading

Ephesians 6:10-17 (CEB)

Finally, be strengthened by the Lord and his powerful strength. Put on God's armor so that you can make a stand against the tricks of the devil. We aren't fighting against human enemies but against rulers, authorities, forces of cosmic darkness, and spiritual powers of evil in the heavens. Therefore, pick up the full armor of God so that you can stand your ground on the evil day and after you have done everything possible to still stand. So stand with the belt of truth around your waist, justice as your breastplate, and put shoes on your feet so that you are ready to spread the good news of peace. Above all, carry the shield of faith so that you can extinguish the flaming arrows of the evil one. Take the helmet of salvation and the sword of the Spirit, which is God's word.

Reflection

The reflections this week have so far focused on relationships across difference. In our rapidly changing twenty-first century, the ability to navigate cross-cultural interactions is undeniably helpful. It's a skill set that prompts us to ask important questions, such as "How can we become more aware of our cultural assumptions? How can we build meaningful relationships with those who have different experiences, memories, and values?"

Yet, as faithful stewards of the gospel, we must not limit our discussions solely to understanding differences. We must also address the dynamics of power. It's imperative that we explore not only how to create a racial mosaic, but also recognize the hammers that smash those mosaics. These are the "rulers, authorities, forces of cosmic darkness, and spiritual powers of evil" mentioned in Ephesians. These are the forces that have sculpted our society.

Lasting diversity cannot flourish without justice. When marginalized individuals witness their privileged counterparts responding to their oppression with apathy, the bonds of community fray, and things tend to fall apart. It's like being caught in a hailstorm, only to have someone with an umbrella stand idly by, watching you get pelted. In fact, it's more like being in a hailstorm while the person with the umbrella not only refuses to share but actively pours ice into the hailstorm machine, all while claiming, "I don't see any storm; I'm not getting wet." Such actions obviously erode the foundations of any relationship.

It's crucial for churches, communities, and individuals alike to conduct a power analysis. This involves asking tough questions such as, "Who has historically and systematically suffered oppression in our society? How have economics, housing, healthcare, education, the environment, and the legal system shaped our neighborhood?" This is an essential step in equipping ourselves with the belt of truth.

Undoubtedly, this exploration can be uncomfortable, but it can also result in a deeper and richer community. In our first few years, New City Church launched various neighborhood engagement initiatives. Despite being well-received, these ministries never took off. After some reflection on these failures to launch, we reached out to our neighbors and discovered a sobering truth: Many were battling a lot of trauma in their lives, making it a monumental challenge to even get out of bed, let alone be part of a ministry.

This challenge was especially daunting for people of color, as most of the free and low-cost therapy clinics in Minneapolis were staffed by white people. Moreover, many therapists of color operated outside the scope of insurance networks. This meant that individuals seeking mental health support often had to pay significantly more to find a therapist who shared their cultural background.

In response, we established the Incarnation Fund—a program to support BIPOC (Black, Indigenous, People of Color) community members in accessing therapy, spiritual direction, and nature-based retreats, all fully funded for a year. Participants also meet in supportive cohorts to accompany one another in their healing journeys.

If this sounds like an expensive ministry, it is! However, we have repeatedly witnessed the transformative power of God's Spirit at work through this ministry, mending wounds that might otherwise have remained unhealed. One participant in the Incarnation Fund aptly summarized the impact:

> The Incarnation Fund impacted my relationship with God tremendously. With free therapy for a year, I was able to heal, grow, deconstruct, reimagine, and rebuild my life on a sturdy foundation of belief and community. As a queer, Black, femme, big-bodied person, moving through the world and navigating different spaces that are built on racism and patriarchy, my existence is political; and to stand in my truth each day is a protest.

The success of the Incarnation Fund is rooted in our commitment to cross-cultural understanding and rigorous power analysis. Without this analysis, the program might have been simply described as "supporting those in need of therapy," inadvertently neglecting the significant barriers that some members of our community face. Thanks to our power analysis, we can collectively say, "We encourage therapy for everyone, but the Incarnation Fund specifically supports BIPOC community members."

This discipleship journey has a twofold impact. First, BIPOC community members come to recognize that the challenges they face from operating in society are not their fault and the presence of these obstacles is validated by the broader community. Reciprocally, white members of our community contribute to the Incarnation Fund as a way to actively participate in the mental health journey of BIPOC community members, all while reflecting on their own unintended contributions to the pain experienced by their fellow community members.

Questions

- How often do you think about power in our society? What do you think is the relationship between power and God?

- Review the different elements of the armor named in Ephesians. Which one of those would you most like to receive from God in this season of your life?

Reading

John 8:3-11 (CEB)

The legal experts and Pharisees brought a woman caught in adultery. Placing her in the center of the group, they said to Jesus, "Teacher, this woman was caught in the act of committing adultery. In the Law, Moses commanded us to stone women like this. What do you say?" They said this to test him, because they wanted a reason to bring an accusation against him. Jesus bent down and wrote on the ground with his finger.

They continued to question him, so he stood up and replied, "Whoever hasn't sinned should throw the first stone." Bending down again, he wrote on the ground. Those who heard him went away, one by one, beginning with the elders. Finally, only Jesus and the woman were left in the middle of the crowd.

Jesus stood up and said to her, "Woman, where are they? Is there no one to condemn you?"

She said, "No one, sir."

Jesus said, "Neither do I condemn you. Go, and from now on, don't sin anymore."

Reflection

Whenever we create communities that are made up of lots of different types of people, conflict is an inevitability. It makes sense, right? Each of us brings a unique set of perspectives and a unique history. Coming into contact with someone with a different background tends to mean encountering different expectations and different needs. Conflict is simply a sign that some of these expectations and needs are not being met.

Now, let's start with a fundamental assumption that when conflict arises in a relationship, it is not because those involved are evil or bad. Rather, it is a sign that one or both parties are grappling with unfulfilled needs.

Consider a recent personal experience of mine. My partner and I had a rare day off but had rather different ideas about how to spend our time. I envisioned tackling household chores, while my partner yearned for relaxation. Fast forward a few hours, and we're fighting over the fate of old Tupperware containers. Isn't it apparent that Tupperware is actually a proxy for our unmet needs? Even if we came up with the perfect Tupperware solution, the underlying needs would remain unaddressed. Peace in our relationships, therefore, hinges on slowing down and letting the Holy Spirit show us what is really amiss.

When we gather, particularly when we gather in diverse communities, there will be conflict. This is not a condemnation of those involved, but an acknowledgement that different cultures have different norms and different expectations for how needs are met. For instance, there may be conflict about whether meetings should start on time or when people are ready, whether there should be food present, or whether it's okay for people to argue in front of others. Each culture approaches these questions differently, and within each culture, individuals have their own unique preferences.

Furthermore, we must not overlook disparities in power, such as anti-Blackness, anti-indigeneity, and anti-Global South sentiments. While many grasp these disparities conceptually, churches often display "All Are Welcome" signs on the outside while on the inside everyone looks the same.

When our bodies go into fight, flight, or freeze mode, as often happens in conflict, our capacity to create and maintain relationships decreases. Consider the scripture we read today. A crowd is ready to publicly execute someone. We can safely assume that it was a charged atmosphere. It would have been entirely natural for Jesus to mirror this energy and confront the crowd with aggression. Instead, he crouched down to draw—yes, to draw—even as a mob prepared to bludgeon someone to death. By slowing, by pausing, and by contemplating, Jesus found the space to say the right words to save a woman's life.

Sometimes, like Jesus, we must fight wars with whispers. I feel as if I'm channeling the crouching Jesus when I absorb people's big energy but remain able to avoid getting swept up in the moment. An essential skill for cultivating diverse communities is the ability to endure the heat of conflict without being burned up by it.

I want to be clear that this is not another way of saying "Calm down" or "Be kind." Indeed, urging people to be quiet and polite is a common tool of those with privilege, who would prefer to silence the voices of those they are treading upon. The goal of community formation is not to be polite but to be present. Sometimes, it's entirely appropriate to yell or use big movements and strong language. Yet, the responsibility lies in harnessing that energy like a wave, rather than succumbing to its undertow.

In South Minneapolis, it's common to hear people, often Black or brown people, speak with elevated voices as they're walking down the street. Neighbors, often white, might misinterpret this as a fight; fueled by fear, they might involve the police. But the people speaking on the street are still *present*; they're just yelling. They're still tracking each other's emotions, listening to what the other is saying, and speaking honestly. Sometimes these conversations end with laughter. My neighbors may not appear "calm," but they're not fighting.

Jesus shows us a way to acknowledge the humanity of people, even in the middle of intense conflict. Jesus didn't crouch down and draw to distract himself from the discomfort of the situation—an instinctual flight response. We know this because of what he said afterward. "Whoever hasn't sinned should throw the first stone" is the type of wisdom that confronts the moment by holding up a mirror to those involved. It embodies presence. Part of discipleship, which means emulating Jesus, involves learning how to stay present with those who will inevitably disagree with us and express that disagreement in all sorts of ways.

Give it a try—as we saw in the scripture, it might just save someone's life.

Questions

- When you're in conflict, do you tend to fight, flight, or flee? Offer that response up to God, and discern if God might be giving you resources to "stay in the heat."

- What can you say to people arguing with you when they are not present in the moment? Are there ways you can invite them into presence?

- When have you gotten into a fight with someone who had a different identity from you? What can you learn from that experience?

Reading

John 14:1-4 (CEB)

"Don't be troubled. Trust in God. Trust also in me. My Father's house has room to spare. If that weren't the case, would I have told you that I'm going to prepare a place for you? When I go to prepare a place for you, I will return and take you to be with me so that where I am you will be too. You know the way to the place I'm going."

Reflection

I am blessed to be in community with activists, teachers, community organizers, social workers, and other church people who firmly believe that following Jesus and creating justice are inseparable callings. We do our best to center the experiences of BIPOC, queer, and otherwise marginalized people. Most days, after our worship gatherings, the energy is bright and hopeful. I love it!

But every once in a while, often on a night when I'm not feeling my best, I look out and silently ponder a sobering question: "Will we, in our quest for justice, be able to organize more effectively than the people who seek to destroy us?"

When I say, "Destroy us," I mean that, both physically and theologically. During the George Floyd uprisings, we witnessed white supremacists descending upon Minneapolis, rapidly inciting violence and then passing the blame to the Black community. They possessed resources, communication networks, and sinister tactics, such as hiding gasoline-filled pop-top water bottles in alleys to make it easier to commit arson. Members of my congregation found these water bottles and saw the evidence firsthand.

Beyond the threat of white supremacist militias, what about those who, theologically, seek to erase the identities of marginalized people? What about those who portray a version of God that bears no resemblance to the liberating love we have come to know and embrace, but instead, promises violence against people like us? When we confront the possibility of our own destruction, how should we respond?

The entire chapter of John 14 is devoted to Jesus consoling his disciples as the shadow of the cross crept closer. Jesus faced the prospect of annihilation, and his followers were struggling to cope with that. They may have even asked themselves a similar question to the one I ask myself from time to time. What do you do when the powers-that-be seek to destroy you?

Jesus offers solace, but not through the lens of scarcity or apathy. He doesn't tell his followers to retaliate against the Romans with even greater force, nor does he advise them to forget about the situation and hope it resolves itself. Instead, he chooses the lens of active abundance: God's house has room to spare. In other words, there's enough—more than enough! In fact, we have the presence of God on earth, the Holy Spirit, who will continually guide us toward abundance! However, it is our responsibility to embrace this abundance willingly; it won't be forced upon us. God's grace is more than enough, and we can actively choose to acknowledge that every day of our lives.

When I whisper, "Will we be able to organize more effectively than the people who seek to destroy us?" into the quiet of night, I hear God responding with gentle reassurance:

My love,

Do you trust that I made this world and everything it needs to find healing?

Do you trust that nothing can out-organize my love?

Do you hear the thrum of my dream for creation, where even white-supremacist militias turn their hatred and their gasoline into gardens?

With this trust bracing you, what loving and fierce action lie ahead for your community to take?

Also, maybe eat a snack or drink some water. You'll feel better, dear.

Praise be to God!

Questions

- What is a deep fear you feel about the state of the world? How might God respond with "active abundance" to that fear?

- Where are the places in your community where people are facing destruction? What "loving and fierce action" might God be inviting you toward?

Saturday

by Rev. Dana Neuhauser

Rev. Dana Neuhauser (she/her) is an ordained deacon in The United Methodist Church and the Minister of Public Witness at New City Church in Minneapolis, Minnesota.

Reading

Revelation 22:1-5

Then the angel showed me the river of the water of life, bright as crystal, flowing from the throne of God and of the Lamb through the middle of the street of the city. On either side of the river is the tree of life with its twelve kinds of fruit, producing its fruit each month, and the leaves of the tree are for the healing of the nations. Nothing accursed will be found there any more. But the throne of God and of the Lamb will be in it, and his servants will worship him; they will see his face, and his name will be on their foreheads. And there will be no more night; they need no light of lamp or sun, for the Lord God will be their light, and they will reign forever and ever.

Reflection

Living in Minneapolis, I have the good fortune of being close to many rivers, creeks, and lakes. No matter the season, one of my favorite pastimes is walking alongside one of these abundant bodies of water. A walk along Minnehaha Creek to the spot where it flows into the Mississippi River is my absolute favorite. I like to stop and sit somewhere along the way. Here, I find a moment of solace and stillness, an invitation to pay attention.

I marvel at how the water finds ways around, over, and through potential obstacles. I attend to the lessons imparted by the water about resilience, adaptation, and balance. I seek the wisdom of connection, interrelation, and mutuality.

A walk by the water also directs my attention to the transitional spaces—shorelines, beaches, and banks where the water and land engage in a delicate dance, hosting their own diverse ecosystems. In the warmer seasons, herons and egrets fish, while cottonwood and wet prairie vegetation grow along the shorelines. Otters and beavers make their homes along the banks, and bald eagles soar and swoop near the creek's union with the river.

This ecological diversity, in right relationship, leads to the mutual flourishing of all creation. Yet, this diversity is regularly threatened by pollutants like fertilizers and herbicides. While manicured lawns may please some, a commitment to a weed-free lawn or garden creates an imbalance that the creek and river cannot gracefully adapt to.

So it is with diversity in our communities. When in right relationship, all flourish, but the toxic pollutants that prevail in our society risk hurting many people to make room for the preferences of the privileged few.

If you have access to a body of water, take some time this week and find a few moments to stop and sit. Let your senses come alive to your physical surroundings. Observe the water—look, listen, touch. Feel the vitality of this moment within you—the breath in your lungs, the beating of your heart, the caress of the air on your skin.

Notice the transitional spaces between land and water. Listen for bird songs, seek evidence of other creatures, and savor the fragrances of the vegetation along the banks. Imagine all the ways the biodiversity in that area demonstrates God's gift of diversity in our world.

If you cannot be near a body of water, gather a pitcher of water and a bowl. Take a moment to pay attention and attune your senses to the water. Pour the water from the pitcher into the bowl and listen to the soothing sounds as you pour. Observe the patterns the water makes as it moves and then stills. Touch the water and notice the feeling on your skin.

Take a moment to feel your own aliveness in this moment—your breath, your heartbeat, the way the air feels on your skin.

Finally, take the bowl of water outside and search for plants or animals that might benefit from water. Perhaps water a thirsty tree or offer water to the birds.

No matter which option you choose, remember your baptism as you meditate on the water. If it's safe, touch the water and remember the promises made during your baptism:

To renounce the spiritual forces of wickedness, reject the evil powers of this world and repent of your sin.

To accept the freedom and power God gives you to resist evil, injustice, and oppression in whatever forms they present themselves.

To confess Jesus Christ as your Savior, put your whole trust in his grace, and promise to serve him as your Lord, in union with the Church which Christ has opened to people of all ages, nations, and races.

Remember that diversity alone doesn't lead us to flourishing, only diversity in right relationship. We are called to repent, resist, and serve Christ in ways that bring up into that right relationship with people of all ages, nations, and races and with all of creation as well.

Questions

- Where have you witnessed resilience, adaptation, and balance in creation? What lessons from creation can you apply in your own life?

- Reflect on a time when you experienced being in right relationship with creation. What did you learn from that time about how to be in right relationship with human community?

- How can we practice resistance to imbalances that we see in our relationships, organizations, and society?

Postcolonial

by Matt Temple

When we talk about being the postcolonial church we do not mean that colonialism is over and that we are somehow past it. "Postcolonial" means we acknowledge the reality of colonialism and its indelible imprint on Christian imagination, theology, structures, and systems as well as the harm that it has caused. It also means we continually and humbly evaluate our imagination, theology, structures, and systems and do the work necessary to disentangle God's good news from that of the empire. This is the work that lies ahead for us, and there are many questions we still need to answer.

Sunday

Reading

Luke 24:13-21

Now on that same day two of them were going to a village called Emmaus, about seven miles from Jerusalem, and talking with each other about all these things that had happened. While they were talking and discussing, Jesus himself came near and went with them, but their eyes were kept from recognizing him. And he said to them, "What are you discussing with each other while you walk along?" They stood still, looking sad. Then one of them, whose name was Cleopas, answered him, "Are you the only stranger in Jerusalem who does not know the things that have taken place there in these days?" He asked them, "What things?" They replied, "The things about Jesus of Nazareth, who was a prophet mighty in deed and word before God and all the people, and how our chief priests and leaders handed him over to be condemned to death and crucified him. But we had hoped that he was the one to redeem Israel. Yes, and besides all this, it is now the third day since these things took place.

Reflection

After carrying the last of the boxes down the stairs, I closed the sliding door on the dingy white moving truck and slid the rusty metal latch into place. It was moving day, and as has been my ritual with every move, I walked back up the stairs to make one final walkthrough of the place we'd called home for the past four years. Each room felt like an empty echo, but as I closed my eyes, they were flooded with memories. Gratitude and sadness simultaneously filled my heart. I could hear the laughter of the new friends we had made and see the tears shed with loved ones mourning the loss of friends. I couldn't help but smile as I recalled the milestones my daughter reached in this home. It's incredible how much life can be lived in just four years.

When my family first moved to Chicago, we were full of hope and a limitless sense of possibility, yet we also knew the adventure would be challenging. We carried a profound conviction that God was going to do something life-changing through us. We were going to change the city! But now, as we packed up to move to Dallas, I was wrestling internally about what we had accomplished. Most of what we had hoped to achieve did not end up working out. This was not due to a lack of effort. We poured ourselves out completely. Nonetheless, there were many dreams that had withered and remained unfulfilled. As I watched the city that I love shrink in my rearview mirror, I felt that our adventure had been an undeniable failure.

In the wake of that painful move, I've had time to reflect and walk with Jesus. I've come to believe that maybe we weren't sent to change the city; instead, it was we who needed to change. Something died in us as that season came to an end, and perhaps, that was God's plan all along.

I imagine that our friends on the road to Emmaus felt something similar. They had traveled to Jerusalem with grand expectations. Jesus, the true king of Israel, had come to the city and those well-versed in the prophecies were certain of his purpose. The Messiah was finally going to set things right. He had come to drive the occupiers out of Jerusalem and firmly establish his kingdom—by force if necessary. They anticipated a resounding and decisive political victory, and they were not about to miss their opportunity to be part of this historic moment. However, instead of triumph, they were met with tragedy as they witnessed the death of their king, and along with it, their dreams of a triumphant empire. And *that* is where Jesus meets them, in the midst of their disappointment, as they walk away disillusioned.

Jesus attentively listens to their pain and begins to reshape the story so that they can see the purpose behind it all. It was necessary for prevailing visions of a violent, colonizing God to die. It was time to reimagine a world reconciled to the Prince of Peace, liberated from the grip of faith in a destructive deity. In this new world, the risen God would not to be found on a throne in the center of the city, but in the stories of the people on the margins.

However, this would not be the last time the people of God sought to establish a so-called "holy" empire. Throughout history, from Constantine's conversion to the Crusades, and even to the belief in manifest destiny among white Americans, the church has frequently found itself enticed by privilege and power. It has embraced and worshiped a colonial God who prefers to destroy what cannot be dominated. In fact, the influence of this colonial God has been so profound that few of us can claim to possess a theology or follow a religious practice that has not been tainted by this false idol.

During this Lenten season, we are once again called to consider how we must surrender our preconceived notions about God to the grave so that Christ can arise in their place. It is an opportunity for us to turn our gaze away from narratives of domination and look for Jesus as he walks with those whom society would try and tell us are the least. This season implores us to confront the truth, no matter how painful it may be, that sometimes things must die so that something more in harmony with the (kin)dom of God can emerge.

Questions

- How does the story of the travelers on the road to Emmaus parallel your own spiritual journey? Have you ever experienced a situation where, in retrospect, your initial hopes and expectations did not align with the reality of the situation? How did you navigate that?

- How can the church avoid succumbing to the temptations of privilege and power? How can the church maintain a focus on justice and equality instead?

- Can you think of a personal or societal belief or practice that you believe should be allowed to die in order for positive change to occur? What is that belief? Why should it be allowed to die and what do you imagine rising in its place?

Reading

Mark 10:17-22

As he was setting out on a journey, a man ran up and knelt before him and asked him, "Good Teacher, what must I do to inherit eternal life?" Jesus said to him, "Why do you call me good? No one is good but God alone. You know the commandments: 'You shall not murder. You shall not commit adultery. You shall not steal. You shall not bear false witness. You shall not defraud. Honor your father and mother.' " He said to him, "Teacher, I have kept all these since my youth." Jesus, looking at him, loved him and said, "You lack one thing; go, sell what you own, and give the money to the poor, and you will have treasure in heaven; then come, follow me." When he heard this, he was shocked and went away grieving, for he had many possessions.

Reflection

How do you feel when you hear the word *reparations*? In today's society, this idea is a charged one, igniting strong emotions regardless of where you stand on the issue. It makes sense then that the rich young ruler had a similarly strong emotional reaction when Jesus suggested that this was the path to eternal life.

We aren't told about the origins of the young ruler's wealth, but it's likely that he inherited it. Wealth, and particularly this kind of generational wealth, can often be traced back to the exploitation of others, especially in colonized lands. Colonization has historically involved those in power moving into a territory to exploit its natural resources and its people. Therefore, a postcolonial church must be one that acknowledges and addresses the historical wrongs and systematic inequalities that continue to impact marginalized communities.

In the story of the rich young ruler, this young man seems sincere in his search for a meaningful spirituality that would bring fulfillment to his life. His earnest pursuit should capture our attention. By all outside measures, this man was living the dream. He had everything the empire tells us we need to be happy, yet here he is reaching out to a vagabond rabbi, hoping for answers about why his life still feels empty. Mark tells us that Jesus felt love for him, recognizing his sincerity but also sensing a barrier to his liberation. This barrier could be removed only by an act of selfless faith. Jesus knew, as James did, that faith without works is indeed dead. Such faith is without power and incapable of setting us free. The liberation of both the exploited and the beneficiaries of exploitation can be achieved only through faithful acts of repentance, redistribution, and reconstruction. These are the fundamental tasks of a postcolonial gospel-centered church.

Repentance begins by centering the stories of people on the margins. Holy work always starts with listening, but it never stops there. It entails believing that experiences different from our own are equally valid. Stories awaken our awareness and invite us to acknowledge the impact of historical injustices, harm, and oppression. This allows us to take responsibility for the barriers these actions have created for some and the advantages that they've provided to others. Repentance requires us to remain open-minded, humble, and alert to the unjust systems that are at play. It means that when we uncover areas of ignorance or indifference, we take action to correct them. Repentance is a necessary first step toward building a more flourishing society. However, as Jesus demonstrated with the rich young ruler, this faith must be followed by actions.

Redistribution involves a commitment to equity, elevating the voices of often-ignored teachers and leaders, and reallocating resources, access, and opportunities to rectify imbalances created by systemic inequality. Redistribution prompts us to ask how resources can be used to uplift individuals and communities on the margins and eliminate barriers to flourishing for everyone in our communities.

Reconstruction starts with rejecting a monolithic gospel centered on individualism and embracing a more expansive understanding of sin and salvation that recognizes the interconnectedness of humanity. The empire seeks to exalt independence and individualism, minimizing the role of systemic power. We see this on display when evangelism and the good news are discussed exclusively in terms of individuals' salvation from their own personal acts of sin. This understanding of salvation and sin is based on a narrow interpretation of the Bible. This version of Christianity leaves little room to examine the power of systems (or powers and principalities), how they take on a life of their own, and how they persist over generations. In the context of reparations, reconstruction entails comprehensive and transformative efforts to dismantle oppressive systems, policies, and practices. This work begins by looking internally. How have we participated in unjust systems in our churches, homes, workplaces, and communities? One starting point might be advocating for more diverse representation in decision-making leadership roles within your congregation.

As we journey toward the cross in this Lenten season, may those of us with privileged identities humble ourselves to the call of justice and repair. Instead of turning away in sorrow like the rich young ruler, may we embrace the power of repentance and actively participate in the redistribution of resources. For those of you with identities that society has tried to marginalize, may you embrace the power of your voice, your story, and your experiences. May you recognize the grace in your perspectives and their power to challenge and reshape the narrative of exclusion. Together, may we engage in the work of reconstruction, striving for a world where justice, healing, and reconciliation flourish.

Questions

- How does the concept of wealth and its connection to exploitation resonate with you? How do you see this relating to issues of privilege and inequality in our society today?

- How do you interpret the idea that faith without works is dead? Can you think of examples in your own life or in society where faith or belief alone fell short of creative positive change?

- How can individuals and communities practically engage in the work of reconstruction, especially addressing historical injustices and systemic inequalities? Can you think of examples of such efforts in your own community or context?

Tuesday

Reading

2 Corinthians 12:6-10

But if I wish to boast, I will not be a fool, for I will be speaking the truth. But I refrain from it, so that no one may think better of me than what is seen in me or heard from me, even considering the exceptional character of the revelations. Therefore, to keep me from being too elated, a thorn was given me in the flesh, a messenger of Satan to torment me, to keep me from being too elated. Three times I appealed to the Lord about this, that it would leave me, but he said to me, "My grace is sufficient for you, for power is made perfect in weakness." So I will boast all the more gladly of my weaknesses, so that the power of Christ may dwell in me. Therefore I am content with weaknesses, insults, hardships, persecutions, and calamities for the sake of Christ, for whenever I am weak, then I am strong.

Reflection

As Christians, it's important to think deeply and discern where we should connect and identify with our society and where we must stand in contrast to it. Nowhere is this more important than when it comes to questions about power. Recently, I watched a documentary about a prominent evangelical megachurch with global influence. The documentary exposed disturbing incidents of sexual and financial misconduct that arose from a flagrant lack of accountability and gross abuses of power from the church's charismatic leaders. Such scandals not only damage the credibility of the church, but also leave a trail of deeply wounded people in their wake. Jesus tells us that a good shepherd will leave the ninety-nine and go after the one, emphasizing the importance of caring for those on the outside. Yet, it seems our focus as a church often centers on the majority, not the marginalized.

When I sat down to write today's reflection, I wondered if I should even reference this recent megachurch scandal, as its relevance might diminish over time. However, the sad reality is that whether you are reading this in 2024 or in 2044, there will likely be a church or network of churches struggling with similar issues. Throughout our history, the church has often succumbed to the allure of power.

A vital lesson we can learn from the colonial era of the church, known as Christendom, is that aligning with status, wealth, or power rarely helps us spread the good news, and it never ends well. When Christianity becomes intertwined with political or societal power, therefore becoming the imposed and enforced religion of the culture, it shifts from being a source of revolution and life to an institution bent on protecting its privileged position. Leslie Newbigin, in his book, *The Gospel in a Pluralist Society* says, "When the Church tries to embody the rule of God in the forms of earthly power it may achieve that power, but it is no longer a sign of the kingdom." As we read in 2 Corinthians 12:9, the power of God's (kin)dom, a power that seeks the flourishing of all, is not made perfect in strength, but in weakness. The places where God's power is on display are likely not the places that attract the gaze of society's elite.

Regrettably, even within the church, the majority of "success stories" we hear are deemed successes only by our society's distorted definition of power. The same can be said for the chorus of voices telling us what a "good leader" looks like. The qualities implicitly encouraged in these stories revolve around independence, competition, command, authority, exploitation, domination, conquest, control, a drive for individual success, siloed thinking, consolidated power, and productivity. These are the hallmarks of the empire, and when God's people seek to mimic them, it rarely ends well. Although they may seem effective in achieving short-term success and growth, they do not reflect the fruits of the Spirit and rarely result in something that lasts. Despite this reality, the temptation to highlight and celebrate these stories and develop systems and structures that perpetuate them is hard for us to resist.

The postcolonial church recognizes that God's power is most potent at the margins. Consequently, we challenge the status quo and amplify the voices and stories that society tends to suppress. We have the responsibility to conduct regular power analyses to assess whether our paradigms of power, hierarchical structures, leadership representation, and celebrated leadership traits line up with God's vision for the world, or if they merely reflect the latest trends promising us success through growth. The postcolonial church strives to emphasize and embody repentance, collaboration, contextualization, vulnerability, long-term vision, aesthetics, compassion, constructive feedback, relationships, participation, sustainability, and empathy.

During this Lenten season, let us actively engage in ongoing self-reflection and examine our attitudes and assumptions about power. May we align ourselves with the teachings of Jesus, acknowledging that true power resides in qualities like empathy, humility, and vulnerability. Let us actively resist the allure of the empire, which entices us to adopt oppressive narratives of colonization, offering a vision of success that ultimately brings only pain and brokenness.

Questions

- How do you define power and what role does it play in your relationships, work, or community involvement?

- Today's reflection contrasts the qualities celebrated by society as hallmarks of power with the qualities associated with the postcolonial church. Which set of qualities do you find more aligned with your values and beliefs? Why?

- How can you engage in self-reflection and examine your own attitudes and assumptions about power? What practices or actions can help you align more closely with the teachings of Jesus regarding power and humility?

Wednesday

Reading

Revelation 21:1-5a

Then I saw a new heaven and a new earth, for the first heaven and the first earth had passed away, and the sea was no more. And I saw the holy city, the new Jerusalem, coming down out of heaven from God, prepared as a bride adorned for her husband. And I heard a loud voice from the throne saying,

> "See, the home of God is among mortals.
> He will dwell with them;
> they will be his peoples,
> and God himself will be with them and be their God;
> he will wipe every tear from their eyes.
> Death will be no more;
> mourning and crying and pain will be no more,
> for the first things have passed away."

And the one who was seated on the throne said, "See, I am making all things new."

Reflection

I recently had the honor of visiting Zion United Methodist Church in North Las Vegas, a historic church that dates back to 1917 and is the oldest United Methodist Church in the Las Vegas Valley. Founded by a group of African Americans from the area who were seeking a place of worship, Zion's story resonates deeply with their enduring commitment to their community.

Upon arrival at Zion, we first explored an empty plot of land covered in rocks and debris that sits on the Zion property. The land had previously held Zion's sanctuary before it was destroyed in a devastating fire. In a world that prioritizes numbers and growth, conventional wisdom would dictate that the church rebuild the sanctuary. Zion, however, took a different path and opted to repurpose another section of their building for worship and redirect their resources in ways to better serve their community.

One remarkable outcome of this decision is the Garden Oasis tended by Mr. Johnny Hampton, Zion's Master Gardener. Johnny was made for this. Johnny radiates an infectious joy and a clear passion for his work that I found moving.

The Garden Oasis is all about the community. It features a farmers market where locals can buy fresh produce harvested from the urban farm. Zion also offers classes for neighbors and community members interested in learning how to grow their own produce, providing an opportunity to rent a raised garden bed for practice. This 3,000-square-foot oasis boasts twelve fruit and nut trees, eighteen grapevines, a variety of fruits and vegetables, and a walking trail along the perimeter so everyone can enjoy this desert sanctuary. To top it off, the garden uses solar panels for energy and resource-efficient irrigation systems for water conservation, pest management, and lighting. Zion plans to build a greenhouse and use aquaponics to expand their growing capability.

In Revelation 21, the writer paints a beautiful picture of our world aligning with God's vision. This is a picture of a new city, the city of Zion. As I contemplate the story of Zion United Methodist Church alongside the picture of Zion found in Revelation 21, verse 22 particularly resonates with me, "I saw no temple in the city, for its temple is the Lord God the Almighty and the Lamb." The work and imagination of Zion United Methodist Church are a living parable of a postcolonial church.

What do we do when our places of worship no longer fulfill their traditional roles as spiritual centers for the people in our communities? The postcolonial church is one where we must reimagine the role that our places of worship play in how we live out the good news. Resurrection takes place only after death. Though we grieve the loss, we embrace the boundless possibilities on the other side. This is at the heart of our faith. Lent invites us to acknowledge and mourn our losses, while Easter catalyzes our hope. At the cross, grief and hope kiss. Yet, for the moment, we find ourselves in this season of uncertainty, a season filled with holy Saturdays between death and Resurrection. It is a season where we are no longer where we used to be but have not yet arrived where we are going. During this time, perhaps we can follow the lead of Zion and plant a garden in the desert to nourish our community and help people find their way back to God.

Questions

• Lent is a time for acknowledging and mourning loss, while Easter symbolizes hope and Resurrection. How do you experience the tension between grief and hope, especially during times of change and uncertainty?

• How might the example of Zion United Methodist Church inspire you to embrace boundless possibilities and find creative ways to nourish your community and help people connect with their faith?

• Think about your faith community or place of worship. Are there opportunities to reimagine its role in the community and explore new ways to live out the good news? What changes or initiatives could be considered?

Thursday

Readings

Matthew 15:22-28

Just then a Canaanite woman from that region came out and started shouting, "Have mercy on me, Lord, Son of David; my daughter is tormented by a demon." But he did not answer her at all. And his disciples came and urged him, saying, "Send her away, for she keeps shouting after us." He answered, "I was sent only to the lost sheep of the house of Israel." But she came and knelt before him, saying, "Lord, help me." He answered, "It is not fair to take the children's food and throw it to the dogs." She said, "Yes, Lord, yet even the dogs eat the crumbs that fall from their masters' table." Then Jesus answered her, "Woman, great is your faith! Let it be done for you as you wish." And her daughter was healed from that moment.

Reflection

I was raised in an evangelical church where our youth group would go on mission trips each summer. These trips were classic 1990s youth-group experiences. Our days were filled with manual labor, and in the evenings, our drama team would perform either at churches or out on the streets. Looking back, I like to think I was quite a performer. Somewhere, I'm sure there is video to prove it, but I digress.

One summer, after a performance at a church, we offered to pray for anyone who needed it. A man, likely in his mid to late thirties, approached me to pray with him. He told me that the night before he had been stoned. I gave him a big hug and began to pray a prayer of forgiveness for what I assumed was his drug use. However, he stopped me in the middle of my prayer with a puzzled look in his eyes and said, "They backed me into an alley and threw rocks at me!"

In that moment, I realized that while I understood the biblical notion of being stoned, I had never experienced it or even considered that I lived in a world where such an experience was still a reality for someone else. In my world, being stoned had an entirely different meaning, and rocks had little to do with it. This incident underscored for me the significance of our individual contexts and experiences in shaping our understanding of the world. Our perspectives are limited, and so is our worldview. This limitation inevitably leads to uninformed assumptions and biases. This is precisely why we need one another. We were not made to exist in an echo chamber; we were created for relationships. When we move toward others whose experiences differ from our own, listen to their stories, and genuinely believe them, our understanding of the world and our Creator expands.

The interpretations of the story of Jesus and the Canaanite woman that I encountered while I was growing up always felt disingenuous to me. If we're not careful, we can easily elevate Jesus' divinity and downplay his humanity. In Luke 2:52, we're told that Jesus, like all of us, gained wisdom as he grew older. Jesus was a product of his culture and his context, just as we are. He developed his understanding of the world from his family and his community in northern Galilee. It's conceivable then that Jesus, being shaped by his time and cultural surroundings, may have held certain assumptions or prejudices toward Gentiles. We must ask ourselves why we are afraid to entertain such possibilities.

This Canaanite woman, like many others Jesus met, asked for mercy, and he initially ignored her. But she persisted, seemingly triggering his internal biases. He appears annoyed, essentially calling her a "dog." Yet this woman refuses to surrender her voice. Her very existence and persistence are acts of resistance. Her determination, self-acceptance, and self-love are a catalyst and inspiration for Jesus' transformation. Somewhere in their interaction, she transforms from someone seeking Jesus' charity into his teacher. Could it be that in this encounter, she exposed a bias that Jesus had picked up from his childhood? Is it possible that the Holy Spirit used this woman as the rabbi's rabbi? You might find this notion heretical because it seems to suggest that Jesus was a sinner, but that's not necessarily the case.

I believe that having a limited worldview, misunderstandings, wrong assumptions, and biases are part of the human experience. We can only know what we know. Our personal experiences and contexts serve as our ultimate authorities in understanding and interpreting the world. Having a bias, in and of itself, is not a moral failing. However, when your bias is exposed, and you choose to do nothing about it, that's a different story altogether. Engaging in this sort of dialogue is essential for the process of decolonizing the church. We need folks with the courage to embrace their identities and celebrate their worth, thereby exposing misunderstandings and biases. We must learn to listen and believe the stories of people whose experiences and contexts differ from our own. When we do so, our perception of the world expands, and God becomes so much more beautiful.

During this season, may you know that God sees you. May you know that your identities and experiences are not flaws to be corrected but sources of strength that can spark transformation. Together, may we learn how to open ourselves to hear the stories of others and believe them. Who knows, we might discover teachers who can expand our faith in some unexpected places.

Questions

- Can you identify an area of your life where you've made uninformed assumptions or held biases because of your limited worldview?

- How do you feel about the idea that Jesus may have had biases? Why do you think this concept can be challenging for some people to accept?

- During this season of reflection, how can you practice openness to hearing the stories of others and embracing the worth of diverse identities and experiences? What steps can you take to cultivate a more inclusive and empathetic perspective?

Reading

Psalm 137:1-4

> By the rivers of Babylon—
>> there we sat down, and there we wept
>> when we remembered Zion.
> On the willows there
>> we hung up our harps.
> For there our captors
>> asked us for songs,
>> and our tormentors asked for mirth, saying,
>> "Sing us one of the songs of Zion!"
>
> How could we sing the Lord's song
>> in a foreign land?"

Jeremiah 29:4-7

Thus says the LORD of hosts, the God of Israel, to all the exiles whom I have sent into exile from Jerusalem to Babylon: Build houses and live in them; plant gardens and eat what they produce. Take wives and have sons and daughters; take wives for your sons, and give your daughters in marriage, that they may bear sons and daughters; multiply there, and do not decrease. But seek the welfare of the city where I have sent you into exile, and pray to the Lord on its behalf, for in its welfare you will find your welfare.

Reflection

Our brains are incredible machines, continuously processing thousands of bits of information every second. When the information seems important, it rises to the surface of our consciousness. Yet, most of this mental activity takes place behind the scenes, unnoticed. To function efficiently, our brains thrive on recognizable and consistent patterns. This reliance on patterns is how biases, as discussed yesterday, take root and why change often feels so hard. When life flows smoothly, our patterns and assumptions remain unchallenged. However, change disrupts these patterns, forcing our brain to adapt.

In recent years, I have found a lot in Psalm 137 that resonates with me. In this song, the children of Israel wrestle with seismic changes in their lives and yearn for a return to the way things used to be. Historically, this psalm was written just after Babylon invaded Jerusalem, leading to the exile of thousands. The people had lost their privileged position in the world. Their temple, which was the focal point of their faith and worship, lay in ruins, and they were left trying to figure out what it meant to be God's people in this new world. Many built enclaves outside the city, hoping for rescue, viewing the current culture as the enemy. Does this resonate with you?

A postcolonial church is not only a rejection of colonial practices and an act of repentance for our involvement in them, but it is also an acknowledgement that our contemporary culture has rejected these actions of the church as hurtful and problematic. I think a quote attributed to Mahatma Gandhi captures this brilliantly, "I like your Christ, I do not like your Christians. Your Christians are so unlike your Christ."

It's intriguing to note that in this psalm, the Babylonians asked for a song, but God's people had hung up their harps and refused to sing. They struggled to adapt to the changes and instead responded with fear and violence. In Jeremiah 29, God challenges the people to alter their perspective. They are not merely victims of an evil culture; they are servants of a loving creator sent into this moment of history to expand the boundaries of who received the good news. They were called to be co-creators, using their imaginations to be a blessing to the people they were sent to. They needed to let go of the way things were and embrace the new possibilities, being people of faith for the world as it is, not as it was.

When we talk about being a postcolonial church, we don't mean that colonialism is a thing of the past. Rather, we acknowledge its indelible imprint on Christian imagination, theology, structures, and systems, as well as the harm it has caused. Being postcolonial means committing ourselves to continually and humbly evaluating our imagination, theology, structures, and systems and disentangling God's good news from the narrative of the empire. This is the work that lies ahead, and there are many questions still to answer. The following list is by no means comprehensive but can help us get started.

1) How has colonization cost us personally and collectively in terms of who God has called us to be and how God envisions flourishing in the world?

Flourishing can exist only when it exists for all. We have yet to fully understand the weight and costs creation has paid as a consequence of colonization. Understanding this cost is essential for us to move forward, identify the changes we need to make, and avoid repeating our mistakes.

2) How does our pursuit and use of power align with Jesus' teachings and his way of life?

For those with privilege, this question should lead you to evaluate the ways you may take up space with your power. You may need to re-evaluate how you wield power, letting some things go, and prioritizing equity, inclusion, and flourishing for all. For those with marginalized identities, this question might challenge you to reclaim some things and dismantle internalized oppressive narratives.

3) What kind of representation exists in our everyday spaces?

This boils down to how much we are seeking to embody the beautiful mosaic of creation. If you throw a party, go out for dinner with some friends, or have people over on a Friday night, who is present? Does your circle of relationships look and act just like you?

4) How can we decolonize our measures of success, both individually and as a community?

How do you measure success as an individual? When you evaluate your week, are the characteristics reflective of a decolonized worldview? What are our metrics for health and effectiveness as a faith community?

It may be time for us to do an honest assessment about the things we are celebrating, using a postcolonial lens.

5) What does it mean to decolonize our spiritual practices?

What we practice on a regular basis determines who we become. If our structures and theology have been corrupted by colonialism, then we must assume that our current spiritual practices have been as well. While this is not a call to abandon historical Christian practices, we should critically examine them and consider how to incorporate new practices or reimagine existing ones in light of a postcolonial understanding of our faith.

During this time of Lent, I encourage you to embrace these questions and others like them. This is how we begin to do the work of building a postcolonial church, one that continuously seeks transformation and renewal in the light of God's love and justice.

Questions

- When have you encountered moments where fear and resistance prevented you from embracing change or new possibilities?

- How do you perceive the impact of colonialism on your faith community or faith tradition? In what ways has colonialism influenced your understanding of God and the church?

- How do you currently measure success in your life, both individually and as part of a faith community? Are there metrics that need to be reevaluated or adjusted to promote equity, inclusion, and flourishing for all?

Reading

Psalm 146:7b-9

> The LORD sets the prisoners free;
>> the LORD opens the eyes of the blind.
> The LORD lifts up those who are bowed down;
>> the LORD loves the righteous.
> The LORD watches over the strangers;
>> he upholds the orphan and the widow,
>> but the way of the wicked he brings to ruin.

Reflection

Start by making a list of words that stood out to you from this week of reflections. Include various nouns, verbs, adjectives, and adverbs that caught your attention or that you were inspired to think about while working through the readings this week. Here are some examples:

- Nouns: empire, oppression, pain, erasure, colonization, liberation, justice, reconciliation, privilege, repentance, solidarity, transformation
- Verbs: dismantle, confront, heal, liberate, empower, reconcile, resist, envision, internalize
- Adjectives: destructive, oppressive, exclusionary, decolonial, prophetic, inclusive, subversive, transformative, courageous, hopeful, radical
- Adverbs: boldly, passionately, compassionately, prophetically, diligently, intentionally, courageously

Next, write out a prayer made up of sentences and phrases with blanks that indicate the type of word needed (for example, noun, verb, adjective, adverb). If you're having trouble envisioning this, take a look at the example below to guide you.

Compassionate and just Creator,

In this sacred space of prayer, I come as part of the diverse mosaic of Christians from around the world. I recognize the _____ (adjective) systems that have sought to erase the humanity of so many. I lament the pain and suffering endured by _____ (group/ community), whose voices have been silenced and experiences disregarded for far too long.

In this season of reflection and transformation, I humbly seek forgiveness for my own _____ (verb) in perpetuating these _____ (adjective) systems. Open my eyes to the ways in which I have benefited from privilege and/or internalized oppression. Grant me the courage to use my voice, platforms, and resources to _____ (verb) as we seek to decolonize our faith.

I repent for the times I have turned a blind eye to the _____ (adjective) injustices faced by our _____ (noun) siblings. Fill me with righteous anger, prompting me to actively participate in dismantling the walls of _____ (noun) and paving the way for a society built on equity, dignity, and justice.

In this lament and prophetic promise, I pray for a world where all voices are heard, where every life is esteemed and valued, and where all barriers are dismantled. May my prayer be joined with thousands of others and serve as a catalyst for tangible change as we strive for a society that reflects your vision of a _____ (adjective) kin-dom.

In unity and solidarity, I offer this prayer, knowing that you hear the cries of the oppressed and empower us to become agents of transformation.

Amen.

Questions

- What specific words or phrases from the prayer exercise resonated with you the most? In what ways have you encountered or been affected by the issues mentioned in the exercise (for example, oppression, privilege, injustice)?

- What steps can you take to raise your awareness of social issues, systems, and structures that exclude or marginalize others?

Equity

By Candace Lewis

This week, we turn our attention to questions of equity. In these reflections, we'll explore the importance of intervening in inequitable situations, the role of individuals in creating equitable change, and the transformative power of supportive communities. More importantly, we'll focus on the need for systemic change and why it is essential to align our words with our actions as we work to create a more just and equitable world.

Sunday

Reading

Acts 4:32-37

Now the whole group of those who believed were of one heart and soul, and no one claimed private ownership of any possessions, but everything they owned was held in common. With great power the apostles gave their testimony to the resurrection of the Lord Jesus, and great grace was upon them all. There was not a needy person among them, for as many as owned lands or houses sold them and brought the proceeds of what was sold. They laid it at the apostles' feet, and it was distributed to each as any had need. There was a Levite from Cyprus, Joseph, to whom the apostles gave the name Barnabas (which means "son of encouragement"). He sold a field that belonged to him, then brought the money and laid it at the apostles' feet.

Acts 5:1-11

But a man named Ananias, with the consent of his wife Sapphira, sold a piece of property; with his wife's knowledge, he kept back some of the proceeds and brought only a part and laid it at the apostles' feet. "Ananias," Peter asked, "why has Satan filled your heart to lie to the Holy Spirit and to keep back part of the proceeds of the land? While it remained unsold, did it not remain your own? And after it was sold, were not the proceeds at your disposal? How is it that you have contrived this deed in your heart? You did not lie to us but to God!" Now when Ananias heard these words, he fell down and died. And great fear seized all who heard of it. The young men came and wrapped up his body, then carried him out and buried him.

After an interval of about three hours his wife came in, not knowing what had happened. Peter said to her, "Tell me whether you and your husband sold the land for such and such a price." And she said, "Yes, that was the price." Then Peter said to her, "How is it that you have agreed together to put the Spirit of the Lord to the test? Look, the feet of those who have buried your husband are at the door, and they will carry you out." Immediately she fell down at his feet and died. When the young men came in they found her dead, so they carried her out and buried her beside her husband. And great fear seized the whole church and all who heard of these things.

Reflection

Trigger warning: domestic violence.

The other day, I found myself at my local Walmart for a quick errand. As I approached the automatic doors, I noticed a distressing scene. The doors were blocked by a couple engaged in a heated argument. As their voices grew louder, the man began to get physical with the woman.

Yet, as all this happened, I couldn't help but notice the reaction of the people passing by. Instead of intervening or showing concern, they awkwardly maneuvered to the opposite side of the entrance, pretending not to notice the escalating situation. As I approached the door, I watched as the man slammed the woman into one side of the automatic doors and began screaming in her face. Yet still, one after another, people walked by. I immediately found a security guard stationed near the entrance. He promptly stepped in as a referee and called for backup.

Why am I sharing this violent, unsettling story from my local Walmart? Because it raises important questions about our role as good citizens. This is particularly true of us as believers. We must ask ourselves who deserves a polite, decent, and equitable society. We must reflect on how often we slide by acts of violence in our society, allowing them to persist unchallenged.

In Acts 4:32-37, we find a vivid depiction of what equitable society looked like in the early Christian community and who deserved to live in such a society. In this account, we see a society characterized by equity, where possessions were shared without distinction based on wealth, race, or identity. Instead, we see a community united by their faith in God, and we see God's grace powerfully at work in the people.

As a result, there are no needy people within the community, and there is a noticeable absence of violence caused by the self-interest of others.

On the flip side, we see the story of Ananias and Sapphira, who, while given the opportunity to be truthful, chose dishonesty and faced dire consequences. Both people were given the chance to be honest about their actions, yet both chose dishonesty, resulting in their deaths. This story serves as a stark reminder to examine our own actions and involvement in situations that lack equity. Do our actions promote fairness and justice, or do we, like those who passed by the violent dispute, prioritize self-interest, perpetuating need and violence in our society?

Let us reflect on these lessons from Acts and strive to create a society where justice, fairness, and compassion prevail, leaving no room for the darkness of dishonesty and violence.

Questions

- What is the definition of "equitable"?

- What would it mean to approach conflicts and conversations at work, at home, and in relationships, by first asking, "Is this equitable?"

- How can you begin to practice being equitable in your everyday life?

Reading

Matthew 20:1-16 (NIV)

"For the kingdom of heaven is like a landowner who went out early in the morning to hire workers for his vineyard. He agreed to pay them a denarius for the day and sent them into his vineyard.

"About nine in the morning he went out and saw others standing in the marketplace doing nothing. He told them, 'You also go and work in my vineyard, and I will pay you whatever is right.' So they went.

"He went out again about noon and about three in the afternoon and did the same thing. About five in the afternoon he went out and found still others standing around. He asked them, 'Why have you been standing here all day long doing nothing?'

"'Because no one has hired us,' they answered.

"He said to them, 'You also go and work in my vineyard.'

"When evening came, the owner of the vineyard said to his foreman, 'Call the workers and pay them their wages, beginning with the last ones hired and going on to the first.'

"The workers who were hired about five in the afternoon came and each received a denarius. So when those came who were hired first, they expected to receive more. But each one of them also received a denarius. When they received it, they began to grumble against the landowner. 'These who were hired last worked only one hour,' they said, 'and you have made them equal to us who have borne the burden of the work and the heat of the day.'

"But he answered one of them, 'I am not being unfair to you, friend. Didn't you agree to work for a denarius? Take your pay and go. I want to give the one who was hired last the same as I gave you. Don't I have the right to do what I want with my own money? Or are you envious because I am generous?'

"So the last will be first, and the first will be last."

Reflection

This parable reminds of the ongoing debate surrounding student loan forgiveness. It reflects the tension between two perspectives. On one hand are those without student loans, who have either already paid them off or had parents who bore the financial burden of their education. These individuals are similar to those who started work in the vineyard early and who had "borne the burden of the work and heat of the day." On the other hand, the latecomers to the vineyard represent the millions of Americans who aspired to pursue higher education but lacked the means to do so without accumulating significant debt. They have also borne the burden of societal responsibility, but without the same advantages.

Both groups are diligently working to fulfill their social responsibilities, yet they have not had equal opportunities or circumstances. The argument arises: should those who faced different challenges be "made . . . equal to [those] who have borne the burden of the work and the heat of the day," simply because they were hired later in the day?

The generous vineyard owner symbolizes the opportunity for equitable action. While it may appear unfair to some, this approach has the potential to alleviate the societal burden of many and enhance their financial security, benefiting everyone. By recruiting the workers who were still available and paying them a fair wage, the vineyard owner effectively contributes to the betterment of society as a whole. As a result, there is less need and more people feel comfortable and secure in their place in the economy. Thus, though it may seem unjust to the early morning workers in the vineyard, the positive impact extends far beyond the vineyard itself.

Between our readings today and yesterday, we have seen how the principle of equity can completely change how we relate to one another and have a far-reaching impact on our lives and the world at large. I pray that as you reflect on this parable, the Spirit guides you to think deeply about the idea of equity and how it can transform lives and communities.

Questions

- What did you feel as you read this parable?
- What new insights do you have now, reading this parable through the lens of equity?
- How do you see the principle of equity playing out in other situations?

Tuesday

Reading

Micah 6:8

He has told you, O mortal, what is good,
    and what does the Lord require
    of you
but to do justice and to love kindness
    and to walk humbly with your God?

Reflection

Have you ever wondered if one person can change the world? This is a daunting question that leaves us pondering how we can even begin to change complex systems. It's understandable that questions about change leave us feeling overwhelmed, especially when the nightly news bombards us with stories that ignite fear and concern for our loved ones and our collective future.

While this response is understandable, we must not let succumb to these feelings of helplessness. Instead, we must use this as a starting point as we begin to identify the systems where we desire to see change take place. We are not just observers of these systems; we are integral components of them. Many of us occupy places of power. We sit on boards, we serve in state houses and government offices, and we work at companies that shape the everyday lives of people around us.

It's all too easy to become disconnected from the lives and struggles of others, failing to recognize that what may appear seamless in our lives can be a matter of trial and tribulation for others, solely because of how they are perceived in the world.

However, when we remain connected and recognize the struggles of others, we can also spark change. Consider, for instance, the recent moves taken by Fannie Mae and Freddie Mac, two government-sponsored enterprises that support much of the country's mortgage financing. Together, these two companies announced plans to expand equitable housing finance plans, which will make accessible and affordable housing more readily available to underserved communities. The two companies created these equitable plans by acknowledging the racial gap in homeownership and by listening to research about why this gap exists.

In their announcement and a subsequent press release, they shared this striking analysis:

> Many consumers encounter obstacles throughout their housing journey, especially those from historically underserved groups. Across our country, communities that suffered from a discriminatory past continue to suffer a persistently diminished present, with housing at the crux of the divide. 44% of Black consumers and 51% of Latino consumers own homes compared to 73% of non-Latino white consumers. These 29 and 22 percentage point gaps translate to roughly 4.4 million Black households and 4 million Latino households. ("The Homeownership Gap," Fannie Mae: Progress with Purpose)

> "Since the launch of our plan in 2022, we have made considerable progress in identifying meaningful ways to address historical challenges faced by underserved communities, particularly for Black and Latino people," said Katrina Jones, Vice President of Racial Equity Strategy & Impact at Fannie Mae. "When you add the present-day challenges of inadequate affordable housing supply and high housing costs, overcoming barriers to housing can seem harder than ever. But we are committed to making a fundamentally fairer and more equitable future for housing." ("Fannie Mae Expands Equitable Housing Finance Plan," Press Release, April 5, 2023)

Change seems simple when we read about it in a press release. Still, this represents a concerted effort on the part of the people who work for the company and those outside the company who have been advocating for more equitable practices in the housing industry.

While it's natural to initially experience what social science researchers call "learned helplessness"—a state where one struggles to find solutions to challenging situations, even when they are attainable—we now have a new question to ask ourselves: "How can we make this equitable?" This question can help us pivot and lead us to contribute to the betterment of our world and local communities through our commitment to equity.

During Lent, we often focus on our personal behavior and growth. While that is often beneficial, let this question of equity challenge us to think more about systems and systemic change during this season of reflection. Christ did not come simply for the good of each individual in isolation but for the whole world. Jesus calls us to make systemic change and embrace equity in our work for justice.

Questions

- What are your first thoughts when you think about systemic change? Does it feel overwhelming? How do you get past this emotional block?

- What does it mean to consider yourself as an agent of change and not merely a passive observer of the systems in place in our society? How does this affect your views on equity and change?

- What are some ways you can learn more about something where you are not well-informed so that you feel empowered to work for change?

Wednesday

Reading

Isaiah 1:16-17

> Wash yourselves; make yourselves clean;
>> remove your evil deeds
>> from before my eyes;
> cease to do evil;
>> learn to do good;
> seek justice;
>> rescue the oppressed;
> defend the orphan;
>> plead for the widow.

Reflection

I've long been a regular viewer of the nightly news, using it as a way to stay informed about what's happening in my city and the wider world. I've learned to watch with a discerning mind, recognizing that the stories I hear might not always present the whole truth. At times, watching the news can be spiritually taxing. However, there are also stories that renew my hope in humanity. These are remarkable human interest stories and incredible acts of generosity they inspire from the community.

One such story that recently caught my attention was that of a high school teacher and mother of five. She was compelled to flee her home state due to life-threatening domestic violence. For months, she sought positions as a teacher in her new location, but the lack of openings in her field forced her to accept several lower-paying positions. She also sought housing assistance to provide shelter for herself and her children.

The housing assistance, initially created as a lifeline for those grappling with housing insecurity during the pandemic, unexpectedly faced budget cuts. As a result, the mother began falling behind on her rent. Yet her determination, hard work, and effort did not go unnoticed by her community. Her story, through the power of news broadcasts, online streams, and local cable channels, reached a wider audience.

Once her story gained traction in the media, her GoFundMe campaign, which initially was far from meeting its goal of three-months in back rent, exceeded all expectations. The outpouring of support transcended mere rent payments, manifesting as a profound act of faith in the transformative potential of human kindness and equitable assistance.

Stories like these show me the connection between understanding our shared humanity and extending equitable assistance. Equity goes beyond just meeting immediate needs; it's about recognizing that even if these modest goals are achieved, people can quickly find themselves in dire straits once more unless there is systemic change. True equity comes when people give not just to help others survive, but to help them thrive, allowing individuals and families to transition from survival to lasting stability.

In a recent update, the mother shared that she finally received a call back from a high school about a teaching job and she would be starting soon. With this opportunity and the help of her community, she caught up on her rent, even paying the rest of the year in advance to secure her family's housing. She relieved herself of the burden of overdue utilities, childcare expenses, and other housing-related debts that had piled up over time. Finally, she expressed relief and now feels that her family can get back on their feet and with a sure future. Providing her children with the security and safety they had been denied for nearly two years affirmed that she had made the right decision for her family.

Hearing this story and others like it have expanded my understanding of the impact of thoughtfulness toward the significant needs of our neighbors. Such acts of kindness can change lives, and in doing so, ripple through society, reshaping our collective world. When I choose to give or donate, I think about how my contribution will effect change that lasts at least a year and contributes to a better society for us all.

For me, equitable change embodies hope for a safer, more vibrant, and more productive humanity. It has the power to heal old wounds, right past wrongs, and, as seen in the story of this mother, offer individuals a fighting chance at safety, stability, and security. It nurtures a shared sense of humanity and, perhaps idealistically, fosters a shift in how we care for one another as a community and as a society. Instead of feeling like we're losing something, we can recognize what we're gaining in this extraordinary ecosystem of compassion and in an economy of kindness that enriches us all.

During Lent, this story reminds us of the power of compassion and equitable assistance. This season calls us to heal wounds, right wrongs, and foster a deeper sense of shared humanity. Acts of equity contribute to a more hopeful and vibrant world for all.

Questions

- How has your consumption of the news and media shaped your perception of the world? Have you experienced moments of renewed hope through these sources?

- Reflect on a recent act of kindness or generosity that you witnessed or were a part of. How did it bring about equity? What broader impact do you think such acts can have on society?

- In what ways can you personally contribute to promoting equity and systemic change in your community, beyond immediate assistance? How can you help individuals and families transition from survival to lasting stability, as mentioned in the story?

Thursday

Reading

Matthew 22:36-40

"Teacher, which commandment in the law is the greatest?" He said to him, "'You shall love the Lord your God with all your heart and with all your soul and with all your mind.' This is the greatest and first commandment. And a second is like it: 'You shall love your neighbor as yourself.' On these two commandments hang all the Law and the Prophets."

Reflection

There's a particular city in the south that recently faced some harsh feedback from its citizens about the treatment of minority communities in the area, including the Jewish population. This city has a mixed and diverse population, which may not be surprising if you live in a city like this one, but it provides important context to the story. This feedback was a fair and accurate assessment of the situation, documented by local journalists and firsthand accounts shared on a community-driven Instagram account with a mission to make the city safer for all citizens.

The city wanted to show that it was listening and partnered with an organization that had begun to host a series of events billed as, "Equitable Dinners: Setting the Table for Racial Equity." The organizers describe these dinners as "an invitation to real talk, real stories, and real action. A citywide event combining arts, local history, and courageous conversations to inspire positive collective action for moving forward together."

The central mission of these dinners is to cultivate skills that help participants converse with depth, honesty, and mutual respect. These skills empower both neighbors and strangers to make meaningful connections, share stories, and inspire one another to take positive action to move the city forward. The dinners are hosted in homes, businesses, places of worship, and community centers.

One commemorative dinner is set to host one thousand individuals at one hundred tables, scattered throughout the city. Beyond this flagship gathering, each Equitable Dinner revolves around a dedicated host. The host's role is to set the stage and determine a date, time, and virtual gathering space for guests. It's suggested that each dinner have between four to eight guests and guests are encouraged to bring diverse perspectives to the table by inviting friends, family, coworkers, neighbors, and community members.

Each host then guides their guests through three big questions that are designed to bring out personal stories, shared values, and evoke empathetic action. In this inclusive setting, each guest is afforded equal time to speak, ensuring a conversation where no single voice overshadows others. There are no speakers, special guests, or egos at these tables; everyone's voice matters and is given an equal opportunity to be heard. It is an environment where conversations are not debates, but an opportunity to listen and respect each unique perspective.

The ground rules and structure help attendees develop practical skills that make the city better and help the people in it live better together. When I first heard about these dinners, I thought it was a fascinating approach to help people see one another as people. The truth is that we are seldom aware of the life experiences of others unless they interact with us directly.

Think about something that may, at first, seem mundane. A person who commutes to work and parks in a parking lot every day may be oblivious to the frustrations of a neighbor who has to deal with the hassle of metered parking and street cleaning days because that's the only parking available. One day, the neighbor with parking struggles puts up signs for a local referendum about more equitable parking or a sign of support for a local candidate who endorses parking reforms. The first person, who has no idea about these parking issues, might see this as something being blown out of proportion. That person might minimize the experience of the struggling neighbor because it's not a problem that person has had to consider.

That may seem like a small issue, but it's a simple explanation for why these dinners are an exciting approach to get people talking with those who have different experiences. It gives people the ability to talk to neighbors and do more than wave good morning or skillfully avoid one another in the driveway. Instead, people learn that we don't all have the same parking situations and that the citations made by the city are astronomically expensive. This situation puts a heavy financial and psychological burden on businesses and employees in the area. This seemingly insignificant problem becomes a real issue of equity that people can work together to resolve to create a better situation for everyone.

This Lent, as we continue to reflect, may we seek to cultivate the skills that force us to think about the bigger picture. May we stay curious about not only our friends and loved ones, but our neighbors that we don't know yet and the world outside our experiences. May we truly seek to make the world better, safer, and more equitable for all.

Questions

- Would you attend an equitable dinner? Does it feel intimidating? Does it feel exciting?

- Can you think of a time when you initially thought something wasn't a big deal until you learned more from someone with direct experience about that issue?

- What are some ways that we can cultivate skills that help us think about the big picture?

Reading

Matthew 23:23-24

"Woe to you, scribes and Pharisees, hypocrites! For you tithe mint, dill, and cumin and have neglected the weightier matters of the law: justice and mercy and faith. It is these you ought to have practiced without neglecting the others. You blind guides! You strain out a gnat but swallow a camel!"

Reflection

Unbiased, fair-minded, even-handed, impartial, just, unprejudiced, non-discriminatory, without fear or favor—nine distinct ways to express the concept of equity; nine unique lenses to examine the intersection of your humanity with that of another; nine diverse approaches to unlearn learned helplessness.

As Christians, we are taught that all who confess that there is one God, one faith, and one baptism are a part of the family, the body of Christ. As part of this body, we are transformed, and our minds are renewed. To what end? Well, for one, so that we are no longer in bondage to fear. In 2 Timothy 1:7, we read, "God didn't give us a spirit that is timid but one that is powerful, loving, and self-controlled." (CEB)

With this foundation, we have the capacity and spirit to cultivate equitable thinking and practices. So, when the questions arises, "Whose responsibility is it to ensure equity?" the answer lies with those who believe in confronting impossible challenges, those who continue to believe that one person at a time, joining forces with many others, can change the world.

Think about your daily life as an ecosystem, a complex and interconnected system shaping the broader world where we live, shop for groceries, and work. This perspective shifts how we view our humanity and that of others, inspiring us to make decisions, cast votes, and engage in civic duties not solely for our own self-interest, advantage, or privilege, but with equity in mind. For instance, we could zoom out beyond ourselves and work to ensure equitable compensation for all people doing the same job. In the big picture, we might see the eradication, or at the very least, the reduction of suffering caused by systemic racism, sexism, and socio-economic disparities through intentional equity.

Furthermore, we might ponder if this new ecosystem could starve the existing societal construct that thrives on fear and scarcity, often causing us to lose sight of our shared humanity. In fear, we fail to advocate for the well-being of others; and in scarcity, we erroneously believe that our experiences are the only ones that matter. Worst of all, fear and scarcity allow us to rationalize the suffering of others simply because it does not affect us directly.

"Without fear or favor" certainly isn't our current cultural narrative, but as Christians, it should be a part of our baptized DNA. We are the salt of the earth and we are called to be counter-cultural. Our baptized DNA should inspire us to be the bridges, healers, peacemakers, and architects of an equitable society that our world desperately needs.

I am reminded of the Louis Armstrong classic, "What a Wonderful World." Armstrong sings of "rainbows so pretty in the sky" that "are also in the faces of people going by." He talks about "friends shaking hands" and "saying "How do you do?"" while in reality meaning, "I love you." The desire to see people treat one another better is evident in these beautiful lyrics. It's a call to see each person's sacred humanity. When we work toward an equitable society, it is because of the humanity we share. In an equitable society, we are all connected and mindful of how we contribute, take away, benefit, and are made better and safer in this new ecosystem.

May we attempt to be citizens of an equitable society. What a wonderful world we could create!

Questions

- As you reflect on this devotional what words rang true for you? What words challenged you? What actions can you take towards cultivating an equitable society?

- What actions can your church or faith community take toward cultivating an equitable society?

Saturday

Reading

Matthew 21:28-32 (NIV)

"What do you think? There was a man who had two sons. He went to the first and said, 'Son, go and work today in the vineyard.'

" 'I will not,' he answered, but later he changed his mind and went.

"Then the father went to the other son and said the same thing. He answered, 'I will, sir,' but he did not go.

"Which of the two did what his father wanted?"

"The first," they answered.

Jesus said to them, "Truly I tell you, the tax collectors and the prostitutes are entering the kingdom of God ahead of you. For John came to you to show you the way of righteousness, and you did not believe him, but the tax collectors and the prostitutes did. And even after you saw this, you did not repent and believe him.

Reflection

As we close this devotional week, we find ourselves back in the vineyard. I have highlighted learned helplessness in a few of these reflections. My intention was not to shame or condemn but to address a struggle that many of us face—inertia that sets in when we fail to question ourselves, seek motivation, or draw inspiration from scripture to apply the gospel of Christ more equitably.

In today's text, we find two brothers who received a call to action from their father. Interestingly, one initially refused, but ultimately went; while the other said he would go but failed to follow through. Does this not parallel life itself? I think we've all had the experience of being like the brother who commits but does not act, especially in the face of societal pressures. What holds us back? Is it fear, the uncertainty of the unknown, the threat of personal loss, or perhaps the lack of appreciation for the task at hand? I'm pretty sure you see yourself within these question marks. How do these questions affect how you think about the challenges facing us as a society and the ever-pressing need to act? How can you challenge yourself to stay engaged and empowered?

Listen, I get it. I know that I'm piling on more questions while providing few answers, but this is why I find this text helpful. In verse 32, Jesus gives us an example of when the answers needed for action were provided, but we failed to recognize their significance. What's interesting about this text is that not everyone missed the answer or deemed action unnecessary; it was the vulnerable members of society who grasped its importance. These people, lacking the protections and trappings of the religious elite, could see more clearly that this counter-cultural invitation to the kingdom of God had the potential to improve the lives of all, not just the privileged.

What's encouraging here is that vulnerability is celebrated. Jesus emphasizes that those who followed the example and took the counter-cultural path, despite their standing in society, would enter the kingdom of God ahead of those who did not.

This parable serves as a warning.

As we close out this week, let us take this warning to heart and align our words with our actions. Let us craft a prayer that embodies courage, action, and clarity.

God, we turn to you in times of heartbreak, when our resolve is tested, and our faith in humanity and governance is shaken.

We lament the impact of _____ on the vulnerable members of our society.

In the spirit of the prophet Amos, we pray, "May justice roll down like water and righteousness like an ever-flowing stream."

God, I acknowledge _____ that makes me like the son who did not follow up on his promise.

In this, I ask for your mercy, grace, and heart for the strength to align my words and thoughts with my actions. Amen.

Questions

- Are you ever guilty of making empty promises and speaking empty words? What do you think causes you to do this?

- Have you ever found yourself resistant at first but later able to act?

- How has this week been for you? Have you experienced any resistance? Take some time to explore that here.

Contextual

Each of the reflections this week revolves around the theme of *context*. These reflections draw inspiration from the Bible and from personal experiences to highlight the significance of connecting with communities without judgment, embracing diversity, and recognizing the unique contexts that shape our faith journeys.

Sunday

Reading

Acts 17:22-31

Then Paul stood in front of the Areopagus and said, "Athenians, I see how extremely spiritual you are in every way. For as I went through the city and looked carefully at the objects of your worship, I found among them an altar with the inscription, 'To an unknown god.' What therefore you worship as unknown, this I proclaim to you. The God who made the world and everything in it, he who is Lord of heaven and earth, does not live in shrines made by human hands, nor is he served by human hands, as though he needed anything, since he himself gives to all mortals life and breath and all things. From one ancestor he made all peoples to inhabit the whole earth, and he allotted the times of their existence and the boundaries of the places where they would live, so that they would search for God and perhaps fumble about for him and find him—though indeed he is not far from each one of us. For 'In him we live and move and have our being'; as even some of your own poets have said,

'For we, too, are his offspring.'

"Since we are God's offspring, we ought not to think that the deity is like gold or silver or stone, an image formed by the art and imagination of mortals. While God has overlooked the times of human ignorance, now he commands all people everywhere to repent, because he has fixed a day on which he will have the world judged in righteousness by a man whom he has appointed, and of this he has given assurance to all by raising him from the dead."

Reflection

In April 2023, I had the privilege of a lifetime: picking up the gifted and legendary Rev. Dr. Renita Weems from the Denver airport and driving her to her hotel in a nearby city. During our commute, she talked about her recent interest in the Jesus Revolution of the 1970s. This movement, she explained, sparked a spiritual awakening in young adults, primarily because the church embraced them without judgment. This movement left an indelible mark on the Christian landscape, and we can trace its legacy to the development of contemporary worship services that use music reflecting modern contexts.

Times change. Music and culture evolve. When we remain open, when we listen and learn from our community without the lens of judgment or disdain, we unlock tremendous potential for lasting transformation in the lives we touch.

Over the past decade, I've worked as a coach and consultant for church growth, while also serving in full-time ministry. The most common question I encounter is, "What are the top five ways I can grow my church?" I understand the desire for a simple solution, and I empathize with the frustration when I tell people that there's no magic formula for church growth, especially in this post-COVID era where many once-reliable practices no longer seem relevant. Nevertheless, I find solace in the example set by Paul, who excelled at contextual ministry.

Much like the ministers of the Jesus Revolution, Paul listened deeply to the people and places he was called to serve. When he arrived in Athens, surrounded by the grandeur of the Parthenon and the idols honoring various gods on the Acropolis, one altar stood out. The Athenians were so religious that they even made space to worship a god they hadn't encountered yet. Paul's first sermon drew from this local context, aiming to connect with a people who wanted to know every deity. He introduced them to a God who couldn't be contained to any altar or idol because this God is the ultimate source of all creation. He even borrowed from their poets to remind them that, in this God, "We live and move and have our being."

Paul's approach in Athens differed from his approach in Philippi, where he settled down, lived among the people, and worked alongside them. In Malta, he began his ministry by miraculously healing the father of a prominent political figure, showcasing God's power to restore and renew those who are sick. Wherever he went, Paul strived to minister in a way that fit the context.

In my work throughout the country, I've met with churches that are eager to revitalize their congregations by reaching young families, even when the neighborhood's main demographic is sixty-five and above. Others resist engaging in Hispanic/Latino ministry despite residing in predominantly Spanish-speaking communities. Some are enthusiastic about connecting with young adults but are reluctant to establish a presence on social media or adapt the way they do church. Context matters! There are no easy ways to grow the church other than taking the time to understand our neighbors without judgment or a desire to change everything about them.

As Christians in the season of Lent, it's time to listen to our neighbors. What are their hopes, anxieties, and frustrations? What are their perceptions of church, and what keeps them disconnected from a faith community? Start from a posture of listening and learning. This is how we breathe life into post-colonial Christianity within our unique contexts.

Like Paul, may you wander the Areopagus in your neighborhood and discover new ways to open the doors of conversation with your neighbors. May this "unknown God" become known to others as you dedicate yourself to relational and contextual ministry that transforms your community.

Questions

- Who lives within a twenty-minute drive of the church facility? Do you know your church neighbors?

- If you were to meet your neighbors and invite them to church, could they join you without feeling judged?

- How is God calling you out of your comfort zone and into a place of contextual ministry?

Reading

Matthew 28:16-20 (NIV)

Then the eleven disciples went to Galilee, to the mountain where Jesus had told them to go. When they saw him, they worshiped him; but some doubted. Then Jesus came to them and said, "All authority in heaven and on earth has been given to me. Therefore go and make disciples of all nations, baptizing them in the name of the Father and of the Son and of the Holy Spirit, and teaching them to obey everything I have commanded you. And surely I am with you always, to the very end of the age."

Reflection

Let's dive into the context of Matthew 28. Here, Jesus gathers his disciples on a mountain in Galilee for a final "great commission" before he ascends to heaven. These are the guys who had the privilege of witnessing, conversing, and even touching the risen Christ. In verse 17, we learn that, when they saw him, they worshiped him, but still some harbored doubts. The Greek word for "doubt" here, *distazo*, appears only one other time in all of scripture. It's a word that signifies wavering or standing at a crossroads without knowing which way to go. You see, the disciples recognized the significance of this moment; they knew that the physical Christ wouldn't stay with them long. They knew this marked both a spiritual and literal turning point. Would they embrace the authority Christ had given them to go and make disciples of *all* nations, baptizing and teaching these new followers of Christ?

As we immerse ourselves in the context of Matthew 28, several elements stand out. First, it's crucial to note that the Great Commission isn't some type of military campaign. Jesus is not donning the colonizing armor of a conqueror and commanding his armies to undertake a civilization-wide invasion by way of conversion. In fact, in the original

Greek, the phrase "Go and make disciples" isn't a command. It's not imperative. Another translation of Matthew 28:19 would be, "As you are going, make disciples of all nations."

"As you are going. . . ."

I love this because it reminds us that we are all recipients of this Great Commission. We are all called to go about our lives with an awareness of the people we meet and how we might shape their understanding of Christ. *As you are going* to work or the park or the grocery store or the doctor's office or the bus station, you are called to make disciples. The process of discipleship unfolds within our everyday lives and relationships.

However, we are also called to make disciples of *all* nations. If we look at our circles of friends or the local communities that we inhabit and discover a lack of diversity, we must pause and reflect. It will be hard to live out the Great Commission in such a context. To be clear, the Great Commission isn't a call to relocate to the remote places in the world or to continue in the colonizing traditions of Christian history, but it is a reminder that homogenous living is incongruent with the gospel of Christ.

This brings us back to the disciples in Galilee, the disciples who both worshiped and doubted. They knew that following Christ wouldn't be easy; it demanded stepping out of their comfort zones. They faced a crossroads. They knew that the path of discipleship would require more sacrifice. For a moment, they wavered, but then each of them followed in the footsteps of Christ. They ventured out into the world, drawing people closer to the love and light of God. They entered unfamiliar and uncomfortable spaces and met new people in new ways. In so doing, they forever changed the world.

So, as you navigate your everyday life, consider this: Who are you meeting, and how are you cultivating relationships that give life to others and bring the kin-dom of God closer here to earth?

Questions

- Think of a recent situation where you felt like you really did not live out your faith in a public space. What could you have done differently? What impact would it have made?

- Think of a place where you typically go on a weekly basis. How can you show up intentionally in that space, ready and willing to share God's love with those who come your way?

- Think about the diversity in your context. How could you open yourself to new experiences, new friendships, and a new form of church that is more diverse and more reflective of what God's kindom truly looks like?

Tuesday

Reading

Mark 16:1-8

When the sabbath was over, Mary Magdalene, and Mary the mother of James, and Salome bought spices, so that they might go and anoint him. And very early on the first day of the week, when the sun had risen, they went to the tomb. They had been saying to one another, "Who will roll away the stone for us from the entrance to the tomb?" When they looked up, they saw that the stone, which was very large, had already been rolled back. As they entered the tomb, they saw a young man, dressed in a white robe, sitting on the right side; and they were alarmed. But he said to them, "Do not be alarmed; you are looking for Jesus of Nazareth, who was crucified. He has been raised; he is not here. Look, there is the place they laid him. But go, tell his disciples and Peter that he is going ahead of you to Galilee; there you will see him, just as he told you." So they went out and fled from the tomb, for terror and amazement had seized them; and they said nothing to anyone, for they were afraid.

Reflection

Did you know that the first gospel account ever written ends in unexpected silence? Did you know that it ends with the good news *not* being told? The original ending of Mark, the oldest gospel, is shrouded in fear and silence. The women discover the empty tomb and hear the reassuring words of a young man in white, proclaiming Jesus' resurrection and instructing them to share the news. But then . . . they don't. They flee in terror and shock, saying nothing to anyone.

Let's look at the context to uncover what might have been going on. Could it be that they were rendered speechless by the shock of what had happened? Or perhaps the fear of societal norms and a patriarchal setting stifled their voices? Perhaps they sensed that their message might not be believed because they were women? There are many possible reasons why the women remained silent, but the precise cause eludes us. However, we do know that this ending unsettled the early church, prompting the inclusion of a longer ending later on.

But what about Mark's original audience and their context? Mark's Gospel was written around 70 CE, shortly after the destruction of the temple in Jerusalem when the persecution of Christians had just begun (although it was not yet widespread). Throughout Mark's narrative, we find a common theme: the messianic secret, where people struggle to fully comprehend who Jesus is and what Jesus came to do.

Could it be that Mark intentionally ended his Gospel in secrecy and silence to draw us into the story, to make his context part of our own? What if, when reading these words, we are meant to feel compelled to respond, to act, to spread this powerful gospel of love? Perhaps we, like the women at the tomb, are still afraid and unsure how the message or the messenger will be received. Yet, the story of God's bold and inclusive love is too potent to be contained.

What if *we* are the authors of the final chapter in Mark's Gospel? What if the Gospel doesn't end with words on a page but with the sacrificial love we express in our lives as we embody the message we've received?

Questions

- When was the last time you showed others who Jesus was by your words or deeds?

- If the early church was editing scripture from the first century, in what ways are you editing God's good news to accommodate what makes you comfortable or safe (or helps you hold onto power)?

Wednesday

Reading

Job 12:7-10

> "But ask the animals, and they will teach you,
>   the birds of the air, and they will tell you;
> ask the plants of the earth, and they will teach you,
>   and the fish of the sea will declare to you.
> Who among all these does not know
>   that the hand of the Lord has done this?
> In his hand is the life of every living thing
>   and the breath of every human being.

Reflection

I'll never forget the phone call I received back in June 2019 from a complete stranger. Her name was Corey; she was a United Methodist pastor in New York, and she had an idea about starting a church at her local United Methodist camp and retreat center in Windsor, New York. Corey believed deeply in our Christian call to care for and connect to creation.

Fast forward to 2020, and Church in the Wild was born. This vibrant community invites everyone to "follow the Spirit through creation, adventure, and restoration." Their core values include being Spirit-led, inclusive, ecologically conscious, alternative, service-minded, margin-centered, communal, and supporters of Sky Lake (the camp and retreat center where they meet).

While Church in the Wild meets for their inspiring "Worship in the Woods" on Sunday afternoons at Sky Lake, they've also embraced digital connection and host regular Zoom meditation groups that coincide with the lunar cycle. They offer monthly Sabbath Life retreats, providing a space to connect with God, commune with others, and renew their bond with creation. Beyond these gatherings, they provide a wealth of other opportunities to gather, grow in faith, and learn from the beautiful natural world that surrounds them.

Corey uses her personal gift for liturgical writing to extend this ministry beyond her community, as she generously creates resources for other churches longing to connect with creation in their Sunday worship. The podcast produced by the community, *Pod in the Wild*, helps others learn from their profoundly contextual ministry and invites others to learn and grow alongside them.

As a community, Church in the Wild passionately advocates for legislative initiatives that protect nature. Their commitment extends to their day-to-day actions and shows a dedication to this contextual faith community and the creation it cherishes.

Long before the pandemic forced many of us outdoors, Corey recognized the growing chasm developing between our society and God's creation. She built the foundations of this faith community on principles and practices designed to bring people closer to their Creator by nurturing and communing with creation. Everything—from their website to social media, their published materials, and their t-shirt fundraisers—demonstrates their commitment to this approach to faith. In the process, Corey has drawn in many people who were not active in a faith community to this new form of church.

Corey's church doesn't revolve around the traditional Sunday morning service or building-centric worship. Instead, this community is reaching out to those who want to blend their love of the outdoors with their love of God. The result has been a fruitful and life-giving out-of-the-box church experience. As John Muir once mused, "I'd rather be in the mountains thinking of God, than in church thinking about the mountains." At Church in the Wild, they wholeheartedly ask, "Why not do both?"

Questions

- Corey found a unique context that she was called to serve. Is there a unique context where you could be serving others in new ways?

- Church in the Wild connects everything they say and do to their driving vision as a faith community. What vision drives your faith community? Are you more focused on *what* you are doing in ministry or *why* you are doing it?

- Are there one or two things you need to stop doing as an individual or as a church to better embrace the concept of Sabbath? God rests; the earth rests. When was the last time you rested?

Reading

John 4:5-9

So he came to a Samaritan city called Sychar, near the plot of ground that Jacob had given to his son Joseph. Jacob's well was there, and Jesus, tired out by his journey, was sitting by the well. It was about noon.

A Samaritan woman came to draw water, and Jesus said to her, "Give me a drink." (His disciples had gone to the city to buy food.) The Samaritan woman said to him, "How is it that you, a Jew, ask a drink of me, a woman of Samaria?" (Jews do not share things in common with Samaritans.)

Reflection

My life was forever changed during my two-year service as a Peace Corps volunteer in Eastern Europe. It not only allowed me to meet new people and immerse myself in a different language and culture but also introduced me to a fresh theological approach.

In most of Western Christianity, we employ what is called *cataphatic theology*, a type of theology that seeks to define who or what God is. We'll say, "God is light," or "God is love," or "God is present." However, there is an alternative form of thought, *apophatic theology*, which is prevalent in Eastern Orthodoxy.

During my two years in Bulgaria, I was able to learn about apophatic theology from people like Nataliya, a friend and colleague at my school. She helped me understand that this theology willingly embraces the mystery of God and is built around the realization that God cannot be contained to a mere affirmative phrase. In this framework, we don't necessarily say, "God is love," but rather, "God is not hate." Apophatic theology beckons us to acknowledge that God dwells in darkness and brings forth light, and we can enter this light of Christ's presence by enduring the dark night of the soul. It invites us to contemplate that God's name in the Old Testament was "I am," which can also be translated as "I am the being one" or "I am the one who was, is, and is to come." Western Christianity asserts that God is present, but Eastern Orthodoxy proclaims that God transcends the bounds of time and place.

This kind of belief holds major implications for us when it comes to the practical side of embracing contextual ministry. What if we didn't begin our ministry from the contexts we are most familiar with? What if we moved away from concrete notions of who our neighbors are?

Consider what Jesus did on his trip through Samaria. Jesus goes to the well for water. He doesn't approach the well during the comfortable morning hours when everyone is present but during the scorching heat of the day, when it lay deserted, except for those who wished to remain unseen and unjudged. In this setting, Jesus engages in his longest recorded conversation in all of scripture. He talks with a woman at the well about her life, her struggles, her sense of identity as an individual and as a Samaritan, and her role in the kin-dom of God. He recognized someone whom society tries not to see, and he talks about faith in a way that was previously unexpressed. In this moment, Jesus shatters social norms and barriers by going into a space inhabited by those who felt invisible and abandoned by others. This is contextual ministry. It begins at the well.

Let us go to the places marked by suffering and social ostracization and simply listen. Let us ask ourselves, "Who is here? Who is absent? What are they feeling? What questions do they have? What are they longing for? What are they celebrating? What do they offer to others?" When we have been present, when we have listened, then we can embrace Jesus' approach of accountability and radical inclusion.

At the end of this story, the woman left her water jar at the well because her life, her body, and her soul were no longer thirsty. Visit the well and witness how Jesus has been meeting the people in your community in that very space long before your arrival. Embrace the mystery of the ways in which God works in places that elude simple description or categorization.

Questions

- List three places you could go to meet those who feel unloved or unseen by the church (making sure to check your privilege and judgment before you enter those spaces).

- Journal about what you see or hear and ask God to illuminate next steps as you move from listening to others to learning from others to gathering, loving, and serving those at the well.

Friday

Reading

Ecclesiastes 3:1-8

For everything there is a season, and a time for every matter under heaven:

> a time to be born, and a time to die;
> a time to plant, and a time to pluck up what is planted;
> a time to kill, and a time to heal;
> a time to break down, and a time to build up;
> a time to weep, and a time to laugh;
> a time to mourn, and a time to dance;
> a time to throw away stones, and a time to gather stones together;
> a time to embrace, and a time to refrain from embracing;
> a time to seek, and a time to lose;
> a time to keep, and a time to throw away;
> a time to tear, and a time to sew;
> a time to keep silence, and a time to speak;
> a time to love, and a time to hate;
> a time for war, and a time for peace.

Reflection

I'll never forget the first time I had to tell someone that he was going to die. It happened during my clinical pastoral education at a veterans' hospital in Durham, North Carolina. I was called in to assist with a palliative care consultation for a veteran in his late sixties. He had just been given the news that his cancer was terminal.

As the medical team left the room, I stayed behind, tasked with helping him process his reaction to this painful diagnosis. With tears in his eyes, this man began to share a vision with me. In this vision, filled with light and love, he was crossing over a magnificent rainbow bridge, entering a place where he wouldn't be in pain anymore. Holding his hand, I listened intently as he continued to share his thoughts and feelings about life beyond death.

As he spoke, something stirred within me for the first time. I was almost twenty weeks pregnant with my first child, and until then, I had yet to experience any flutters of the life within. Yet, as this veteran spoke about his impending death and journey into what comes next, my son showed me a sign of life. It was a profound reminder of the interconnectedness between the seasons of life. Even in the midst of death, the promise of life looms on the horizon.

In the broader context of Christianity, there are many churches and denominations that may perceive themselves to be in the midst of decline, despair, or even death. Yet others feel it is a season to rejoice, dance, or sow the seeds of new ministries. Too often, we find ourselves so busy going through the motions of faith that we neglect to pause and discern what season we are living through and what season God is calling us to embrace next.

As you revisit this well-known passage from Ecclesiastes, take a moment to meditate on the words and write down your thoughts about the season you are living in now and the season you are being called to live into. Ponder the steps you can take to gracefully transition from what is to the promise of what will be.

Questions

- What three things can you stop doing right now to create the energy, time, and freedom you need for the season that awaits?

- What ritual could you embrace to help you name or identify the seasons in your life that have shaped you the most? Could you light a candle, write a letter to yourself, or gather for a meal with friends? What benefits might come from connecting to your own story and the seasons in your life?

Saturday

Reading

Isaiah 42:1-5

Here is my servant, whom I uphold,
    my chosen, in whom my soul delights;
I have put my spirit upon him;
    he will bring forth justice to the nations.
He will not cry out or lift up his voice
    or make it heard in the street;
a bruised reed he will not break,
    and a dimly burning wick he will not quench;
    he will faithfully bring forth justice.
He will not grow faint or be crushed
    until he has established justice in the earth,
    and the coastlands wait for his teaching.

Thus says God, the Lord,
    who created the heavens and stretched them out,
    who spread out the earth and what comes from it,
who gives breath to the people upon it
    and spirit to those who walk in it.

Reflection

The practice of breath prayer traces its origins to the sixth century and the revered desert fathers and mothers. I've grown to embrace this practice more consistently now that I live in Phoenix, Arizona, in the Sonoran Desert. I appreciate this prayerful ritual because it helps me recenter on the breath that gives me life—a breath that many of us took for granted until a global pandemic challenged our collective ability to breathe freely.

I also appreciate the significance of the connection to the way the word "breath" is used in both the Old and New Testaments. In scripture, the word translated as "breath" is often the same as the word for "spirit" or "Holy Spirit," serving as a reminder that God's breath can guide, sustain, and encourage us on the journey of life. It's a beautiful reminder of the divine presence that flows within us.

I'm also grateful for breath prayers because they provide a tangible way let go of burdens. In the simple act of exhalation, we find a spiritual and physical release from the weight of things that we were never meant to carry.

Here's how you can practice breath prayer:

1. **Find a comfortable seat.** Locate a comfortable place to sit with your back straight and your feet firmly planted on the floor. Rest your hands gently on your lap.
2. **Read the prompts.** As you begin, read the prompts below. Inhale deeply, embracing the presence and goodness of God. As you exhale, release any anxiety, pain, struggle, or burden you may be carrying.
3. **Continue in prayerful silence.** Maintain this slow, steady pattern as long as your spirit calls you to sit in prayerful silence.

Now, let us embrace the breath prayer:

Inhale: Jesus, Son of God
Exhale: Have mercy on me, a sinner.

Inhale: Ever-present God
Exhale: May I feel you here.

Inhale: You know me.
Exhale: You love me.

Inhale: You know my neighbors.
Exhale: You love my neighbors.

Inhale: You see me.
Exhale: You see the unseen.

Inhale: Help me to see
Exhale: All your children.

Inhale: God of love
Exhale: May all know your love.

Innovation

Many church folks lean away from language about church planting, starting new ministries, or innovation because of the American church's history of colonization. Even today, many church planting networks aim to "reclaim the neighborhood for Jesus," which is often code for "We want these people to do things our way."

But when we consider history through a last-shall-be-first lens, we find that marginalized people have always had to innovate our ministries. From base ecclesial communities to hush harbors for enslaved Africans to LGBTQ+ people looking out for each other during the HIV/AIDS crisis, there have always been always been subversive, life-saving, innovative ministries expressing the gospel. The gospel has always spurred innovation because the powerful have always oppressed. This week we explore innovation not to find the next shiny thing, but rather to respond to the ways God is guiding us to something new, exciting, and full of life.

Sunday

Reading

Acts 2:42-47 (CEB)

The believers devoted themselves to the apostles' teaching, to the community, to their shared meals, and to their prayers. A sense of awe came over everyone. God performed many wonders and signs through the apostles. All the believers were united and shared everything. They would sell pieces of property and possessions and distribute the proceeds to everyone who needed them. Every day, they met together in the temple and ate in their homes. They shared food with gladness and simplicity. They praised God and demonstrated God's goodness to everyone. The Lord added daily to the community those who were being saved.

Reflection

A lot of truly innovative people don't see themselves as innovators. Your inner critic may look at your own work and experience and say, "I'm not an innovator; innovation is something that happens in big companies that create groundbreaking inventions that change our society. I don't know anything about that."

Innovation is not confined to these narrow boundaries; it resides within anyone who has felt discomfort. For instance, remember that time your radiator was making funny noises and disrupting your sleep, so you rigged a sound buffer out of a blanket and duct tape? Or consider that one day in school when you forgot to do your homework, so you improvised a presentation using whatever you had in your backpack? What about that trip where your restless kids wouldn't stop screaming in the car, so you, like many parents before you, "invented" the quiet game?

See, you're an innovator! In moments of discomfort, when easy solutions weren't available, you created something new. Pain, in fact, compels us all to become innovators.

Think about this in the context of the church. The quickest path for the church to embrace innovation is to cultivate a healthy relationship with and proximity to pain. This approach contradicts our natural instincts. Most people avoid discomfort and prefer communities where they remain unchallenged within their comfort zones. Evolutionary logic reinforces this preference, as discomfort has historically made it harder to live, leading to the development of a nervous system wired for ease.

Yet, when we defy these instincts and move toward pain, especially while praying to God about it, something sacred unfolds. Think about these painful situations and how they might prompt innovation:

- "Everyone in my community is stressed out of their mind and feeling disconnected. What do you think about that, God?"
- "The local middle school cut all of their after-school programming, and a nearby nursing home is looking for musicians. What do you think about that, God?"
- "My church says we don't have time to reach out to people, but we spend three hours every week preparing a weekly worship bulletin. What do you think about that, God?"
- "Research indicates that climate change will disproportionately impact the wellbeing of children worldwide, but my town lacks motivation to do anything about it. What do you think about that, God?"

You can see how innovation naturally arises from well-framed questions asked in conversation with God.

In our reading from Acts today, we witness pain and prayer converging to reveal a community that God loves. Early Christians found liberation in God, and God empowered them to weave together a radically diverse community. However, disparities still existed within this community: some didn't have enough while others possessed abundance. In their prayer, I imagine them asking God questions such as:

- "I don't have any shoes, but my new sibling in Christ has two. What do you think about that, God?"

- "I have valuable land, and some don't even have change in their pocket. What do you think about that, God?"

Innovation continued to unfold. Do you see how this incredible story would not have been possible if the marginalized hadn't advocated for their needs? And it wouldn't have been possible if the privileged hadn't believed their stories. Do you see how God's love fostered enough trust within the community that previously unimaginable sharing became an opportunity for joyful collaboration?[1]

Finally, some may read this and think, "My church does a lot of charity work, so my church is doing a good job moving toward pain in the world." However, charity often covers only half of the story. Acts 2 emphasizes how the believers shared together, how *mutual* their relationship was. The text does **not** say "The believers would sell possessions and distribute the proceeds to everyone who needed them, but only if the people with money could take pictures with the poor to post on social media. Also the people without money had no say about how the organization was run. The rich didn't actually want to disrupt generational poverty; they just wanted to give enough that they could feel good about themselves."

Instead, the book of Acts says that they *shared*. Mutual sharing is what creates change. Mutual sharing is a dynamic that is significantly more challenging to establish and maintain. As I write this, I recognize that, while there are myriad ways I am intentionally moving towards pain in our society, there are even more ways that I am falling into the same patterns of empire that created injustice in the first place.

The good news is that this story transcends individuals; it's a story about God and what God accomplishes through people. None of us can perfectly embody or fully embrace pain, nor can we establish perfect

---

1. Check out Dr. Candace Lewis's devotional on page 70 to read about Ananias and Sapphira, who represent the messiness of the community being discussed here. That story notwithstanding, I am nonetheless struck that the book of Acts records community-led innovation that results in the world looking more like the kin-dom of God!

mutuality. However, when we offer our intentions to God, the Holy Spirit transforms those intentions into innovations, propelling us, inch by inch, toward a community characterized by genuine, joyful sharing.

Questions

- What is the pain that you know best?
- How might God be asking you to address that pain?
- What pain might God be asking you to move closer to?

Monday

Reading

Luke 16:10-12 (CEB)

Whoever is faithful with little is also faithful with much, and the one who is dishonest with little is also dishonest with much. If you haven't been faithful with worldly wealth, who will trust you with true riches? If you haven't been faithful with someone else's property, who will give you your own?

Reflection

A member of our church, whom we'll call Andrew, approached me with an intriguing proposal: "Pastor, what if we bought an empty lot to build a hydroponic greenhouse for our neighborhood?" This idea fit the values of our church like a glove. Hydroponics offers a sustainable way to grow food by creating interconnected ecosystems where plants and fish mutually thrive, and a greenhouse would extend our growing season. This project would also address a pressing issue in our neighborhood, which resides in a food desert due to the legacy of racist zoning laws. It was a compelling vision.

However, our church community was just a few months old. We had promising small groups and occasional events, but we lacked the consistency needed to manage a literal ecosystem. Andrew's proposal asked us to make a significant commitment to a place we hadn't even seen.

In situations like this, the role of a church planter is to steward momentum above all else. We understand that nothing kills momentum faster than dismissing a passionate church member's idea. So, what were our options? Invest way too many resources into something uncertain or squash the dreams of the visionary who came up with the idea?

Inspired by lean startup methodology and books like Ann Mei Chang's *Lean Impact*, Andrew and I started asking crucial questions such as, "What's the simplest, most cost-effective way to determine if this is a good idea? How can gather what we need to know and adjust course accordingly?"

The reality was that buying an empty lot and building a greenhouse were beyond the means of our nascent community; we could barely afford coffee. Moreover, the legal requirements for land acquisition and construction would take as many months to complete as our church had been in existence. So, we set out to explore a smaller, more manageable experiment that could provide insight into the feasibility of the greenhouse project.

In our reading today, Jesus teaches us that "whoever is faithful with little is also faithful with much." This wisdom applies directly to launching new ministry ideas. Let's demonstrate faithfulness with something small *now* instead of spending months planning something that may never materialize. Let's run a pilot project *this month* instead of waiting a year to build a greenhouse.

We identified that neighborhood leadership was vital for the greenhouse project's success. I lived in the neighborhood; Andrew didn't; and neither of us knew someone local who would want to run a greenhouse. We opted to launch a fruit tree program instead. With a wagon full of affordable fruit trees (which cost a mere fraction of a greenhouse), we went door to door, offering them to our neighbors for free. We figured that if neighborhood leadership was what we needed, planting fruit trees could quickly reveal a potential neighborhood leader. Andrew got to breathe life into his idea, and more importantly, we engaged with our neighbors.

The fruit tree program allowed us to demonstrate faithfulness with a little before trying something larger. The program was successful, facilitating meaningful interactions with our neighbors, and we planted dozens of fruit trees. However, despite our best efforts, we couldn't identify neighborhood leadership, a key requirement for the program's long-term success. We started asking our neighbors more questions and eventually discovered that their hesitance to lead a greenhouse project stemmed from their mental health challenges, particularly those rooted in racialized trauma (meaning trauma resulting from racist violence). Many felt that they could barely get out of bed in the morning, much less lead a program. In response, we completely pivoted, abandoning the fruit tree planting and greenhouse discussions in favor of addressing trauma and healing. This shift was *extremely* resonant with our community, far more than any previous concepts we had piloted.

Consequently, we launched the Incarnation Fund,[2] dedicated to supporting BIPOC community members in accessing therapy, spiritual direction, and nature-based retreats. We encourage participants to work with BIPOC practitioners, making it a program *by* and *for* the BIPOC community. Our neighbors do love nature, as we had suspected with the greenhouse idea, but their desire was to interact with nature through healing rather than through additional responsibilities.

From a simple idea about a greenhouse, God led us through rapid experimentation to develop a substantial program that faithfully supports BIPOC leaders in their journey toward self-initiated healing. Undoubtedly, you too have a dream. Why wait? Start now.

Questions

• What is the biggest dream for ministry you can imagine?

• What is a small, fast way to see whether that idea is God-called or simply a day dream?

• Who can hold you accountable to starting soon?

---

2. I discuss the Incarnation Fund in another devotional on page 34. Now you know the backstory!

Reading

Acts 16:13-15 (CEB)

On the Sabbath we went outside the city gate to the riverbank, where we thought there might be a place for prayer. We sat down and began to talk with the women who had gathered. One of those women was Lydia, a Gentile God-worshipper from the city of Thyatira, a dealer in purple cloth. As she listened, the Lord enabled her to embrace Paul's message. Once she and her household were baptized, she urged, "Now that you have decided that I am a believer in the Lord, come and stay in my house." And she persuaded us.

Reflection

In preparation for my journey into church planting, I, like so many others, tried to stuff in as much professional development as I could before I started.[3] Following my time in seminary, I voraciously read around a hundred church planting books, actively participated in numerous conferences, completed a residency at Urban Village Church in Chicago, and interviewed as many church planters as I could manage. It didn't escape my notice, however, that the majority of widely circulated books and well-attended conferences on church planting were primarily created by white, cisgender, straight, upper-middle-class (or upper-class) men. It was, shall we say, interesting.

Yet, as I started talking to people within the Urban Village community, I discovered a stark contrast. Across Chicago, there existed a vibrant tapestry of BIPOC, queer, female, and trans/non-binary people who harbored a profound interest in starting ministries. Among them

---

3. I talk about church planting here specifically, because that is my experience, but my intention is for these insights to be applicable in a broad range of situations.

were community organizers, artists, mystics, and preachers, each pioneering unique expressions of church planting. Some resembled a traditional Sunday morning church model while others forged entirely novel approaches, but they all were church planters nonetheless.

We, the authors of this book, started Intersect because we recognized the disconnect between the widely available resources and our deeply lived experiences. We know that innovation often thrives on the margins of society, and it makes sense for the church to collectively look at how marginalized people continually adapt and innovate so that their communities survive. Simultaneously, it's problematic to assume that marginalized people, who *must* innovate out of necessity, would not also benefit from a range of resources. Intersect endeavors to bridge this gap.

Allow me to share some key insights from my interactions with BIPOC and queer church planters:

1. **Dismantle the Charismatic Superhero Myth:** Contrary to popular belief, launching a new ministry doesn't necessitate being a charismatic superhero on stage. Many in my community, especially women/femmes, have been conditioned to take up as little space as possible, often leading to them being passed over because church planting (supposedly) requires boisterous public speaking and extreme extroversion. While effective communication is crucial, it need not be the exclusive domain of the lead person. What truly matters are relationships that build trust, which can beget more relationships and more connections; "quiet" individuals sometimes are the best at this. Assemble a team that complements one another's strengths!

2. **Be Honest about Costs:** Many marginalized folks I've worked with prefer to bear the cost of their ministry as their personal contribution to the cause. However, the community often remains oblivious to the true costs, whether financial or emotional. This invisible burden can swiftly transform into resentment. It's wiser to transparently name the true costs, then adjust based on the community's willingness to support. Avoid letting people live in a fantasy about what is possible while you suffer in silence.

3. **Clarify Your Non-Negotiables:** When starting on my church planting journey, I prayed a lot about my non-negotiables. These are the fundamental prerequisites that must be true for this to be *your* calling. There are plenty of good causes out there, but not all are your calling. As you develop in leadership, more people ask for help, which will ramp up the pressure. Holding on to these non-negotiables will help you avoid the trap of saying *yes* to everything, and then, upon becoming too busy, having to say *no* to everything. Self-advocacy, as you can tell, is a big theme among all of these.

I like the story of Lydia for a lot of reasons. For starters, Lydia, a woman from Asia Minor, diverges from our modern archetype of a white, cisgender, straight man. She didn't command the spotlight; she wasn't a superhero. What Lydia did have was an encounter with God that was so life-altering that it compelled her to extend hospitality to a group of people. This marked the beginning of her innovative ministry, and she did it so well that she made it into the Bible!

Questions

- How has your social location (gender, race, ability level, sexual orientation, etc.) influenced your relationship with innovation? Without judging your answer, offer it up to God. What response do you hear?

- Who are the "Lydias" in the community that you can support today?

Wednesday

by Rachel Gilmore

Reading

John 10:10

The thief comes only to steal and kill and destroy. I came that they may have life and have it abundantly.

Ephesians 2:19-22

So then, you are no longer strangers and aliens, but you are fellow citizens with the saints and also members of the household of God, built upon the foundation of the apostles and prophets, with Christ Jesus himself as the cornerstone; in him the whole structure is joined together and grows into a holy temple in the Lord, in whom you also are built together spiritually into a dwelling place for God.

Reflection

In 2019, in the heart of Harrisburg, Pennsylvania, the downtown urban churches were in trouble. Ten churches, once vibrant, grappled with large buildings and shrinking congregations. After much consideration, a bold and difficult decision was made to invite all ten churches to merge and become a single United Methodist church, called The Journey.

At the lead of this new merged church was Reverend Kris Sledge, who had previously pastored an established church for four years but felt a calling to become a church planter of a new, unique community. When Rev. Sledge arrived in 2019, The Journey had about fifty to sixty people in worship, with 98 PERCENT of them being white and over sixty years old. Fast forward to April 2023, and there are an impressive 293 members active in the church. Among these, people of color constitute two of every five members, while three of every five kids and youth identify as people of color. Furthermore, two-thirds of the church is under forty years old, with ten percent LGBTQIA+ representation in the church body. So how did this happen? How did this church grow larger, younger, more diverse, and more inclusive—all in the midst of a pandemic? Let's delve into the ABCs of innovative ministry to explain this transformation.

A—Ask questions in your community that no one else has asked. Kris and his core team spent time listening and learning from their neighborhood, acutely aware that they were the only communal space in the immediate area. They discovered a hunger for a church that was both queer-affirming and justice-oriented, coupled with a desire for more contemporary worship and a healthy spiritual environment. During the pandemic, they facilitated community conversations with local and state leaders, addressing the questions closest to the hearts and minds of their neighbors. The Journey has become a place where all are invited to walk together toward truth and justice. Their innovative community ministry was rooted in respect and understanding, refraining from coercive tactics to draw people on Sunday mornings.

B—Belonging matters, now more than ever. The Journey prioritizes people over programming. If they're hosting activities that aren't bringing people closer together in community, they stop doing those activities. Instead of spending time talking about what they're doing, they spend time talking about who they are and how this leads them to what they do. In the process, they intentionally curate an inclusive, innovative community for all God's children.

C—Cultivate the contagious good. The Journey seeks to embrace the message of "contagious good" found in John 10:10. In this passage, we are reminded that Christ came to give us abundant life. In the words of one of The Journey's pastors, "If what you are doing here at church isn't adding value, depth or peace to your life, stop doing it." This church does not insist that people do things that are not life-giving work for them. No one is forced to serve in ways that fill up their schedule while exhausting their soul and disconnecting them from what matters most.

Instead, this church invites people to engage in ministry that is truly good news to those they meet, and there's no shame or guilt to keep volunteering. This invitation to belong and serve is contagious and brings good to the lives of those involved and the lives of those they touch.

D—Don't be afraid to talk about the issues that matter the most. When we seek to reach younger generations, they will expect the church to engage in crucial conversations that matter beyond the doors of the church. They want to talk about racism, climate change, sexuality, addiction, and a wide variety of other topics that have often been taboo in churches. At The Journey, they don't shy away from conversations that cause tension, or conversations that cause joy, or any conservation in between. They are open to discussing whatever is on the hearts and minds of those in their community. In the process, they create space for the Holy Spirit to shape and form the dialogue that is taking place in this faith community.

In essence, The Journey's remarkable transformation from dwindling congregation to a thriving, diverse, and inclusive community can be attributed to their commitment to these principles. They ask questions; they prioritize people; they foster the contagious good, and they are not afraid to talk about the important things. This approach allows them to adapt and flourish in the face of adversity, offering an inspiring example for faith communities seeking to evolve and grow in today's world.

Questions

- Look over the list above. Where could you or your faith community do a better job of engaging in innovative ministry?

- Think about the concept of the "contagious good" and what it means to receive the abundant life that Christ offers. Do you feel like the things you do for the kin-dom of God bring you value and peace in your life? Why or why not?

Reading

Matthew 6:31-34 (CEB)

Therefore, don't worry and say, "What are we going to eat?" or "What are we going to drink?" or "What are we going to wear?" Gentiles long for all these things. Your heavenly Father knows that you need them. Instead, desire first and foremost God's kingdom and God's righteousness, and all these things will be given to you as well. Therefore, stop worrying about tomorrow, because tomorrow will worry about itself. Each day has enough trouble of its own.

Reflection

If you could measure just one thing to tell you whether you were truly following your calling from God, what would it be? Would it be dollars given to the poor? Hours spent in prayer? What about the number of deep conversations about God with people you love?

In my church, one couple created a separate bank account for their "generosity giving." They decided that God had called them to live a generous life. What mattered most to them was using their money in a way that could bless the people in their lives and community. They also knew that simply saying, "I want to be generous" is a vague way of achieving such a goal. It's just not enough. They needed something tangible, something measurable. Now, they can log in to that account, see the balance, and say to each other, "Okay, we have $65 to give away this month."

But what about a church? What should we measure to tell whether a church is following its calling from God?

Church leaders and church planters have a common complaint when it comes to a question like this. You'll often hear them lament that the traditional metrics of church success, attendance and finances, simply don't match their reality on the ground. Again and again, I've heard from church planters across the country, "I hate that all I report are nickels and noses."

And it's true, average worship attendance and financial giving ("nickels and noses") don't have anything to say about the depth of the relationships in a congregation. They don't tell you anything about the momentous life and career choices that have been discerned or the justice that has been achieved for the neighborhood. Counting the number of baptisms doesn't demonstrate ongoing faith development.

Using attendance as the only metric for the health of a church is like using weight as the only metric to measure the health of a human body. There are certainly a number of ways that they're related, but there are just so many exceptions to the rule that the metric is entirely insufficient. There are people who don't weigh a lot, like a malnourished person, who aren't healthy, and there are people who weigh more than most people, like athletes, who are incredibly healthy. Nevertheless, our cultural obsession with the number on the scale has detrimental effects from social stigma to mental health.

Imagine if the abolition-era churches that fought to end slavery were evaluated only on the basis of "nickels and noses." Imagine if the churches that supported the civil rights movement were evaluated only on the basis of "nickels and noses." Imagine if the ministry of Jesus was evaluated only on the basis of "nickels and noses."

Don't get me wrong; I think it's important to measure things. Numbers help us uncover a certain type of truth, detect patterns, and hold ourselves accountable to reality beyond our perception. The tougher task, though, is to identify the things that matter the most.

In our scripture today, Jesus tells us that we should focus on seeking the kingdom of God (or, as folks who want to rid these images of their patriarchal legacy prefer, *the kin-dom of God*). This focus leads us to the most important question. If we are seeking the kin-dom of God, if we are uniting with God to do build this kin-dom on earth, what could we measure that would let us know that we are doing that work and doing it well?

As you reflect on today's scripture, pray about what kin-dom metrics might prove useful for your life or for the life of your community. These metrics should be context-specific, but consider these suggestions:

- Rather than measuring attendance, measure critical mass. Critical mass is the number of people required for a space to feel energized. A worship service with twenty-five people feels good if you're meeting in a room built for thirty, but a worship service of one hundred people feels bad if you're in a cathedral built for five hundred.
- Rather than measuring giving as money that comes in, measure giving by the money that get distributed out. This might mean money given out through direct financial redistribution, but it might also mean measuring how many dollars have been directed to Black-owned businesses or dollars spent paying livable wages to people who otherwise wouldn't have a job.
- Measure key outcomes to the vitality of the community like the amount of art created, the projects that have been imagined, and the partnerships that have been forged.
- Lastly, look for impacts beyond the institutional church—communities fed, soil restored, local economies bolstered, poverty alleviated, homeless people housed, reparations paid, and so forth.

Sometimes simply asking questions about what is most important to us generates enough space for the Holy Spirit to break in. So let's begin counting—counting what truly matters, counting as we work together to build God's kin-dom on Earth.

Questions

- If you could measure just one thing to tell you whether you are following your calling from God, what would it be?
- If you could measure three things to tell you whether your church is following its calling from God, what would they be?
- What could we measure that would let us know that we are building the kin-dom of God?

Friday

Reading

Jeremiah 1:9-10 (CEB)

> Then the LORD stretched out his hand,
>> touched my mouth, and said to me,
>> "I'm putting my words in your mouth.
> This very day I appoint you over nations and empires,
>> to dig up and pull down,
>> to destroy and demolish,
>> to build and plant."

Reflection

Innovation isn't confined to brainstorming and putting post-it notes on a whiteboard; it encompasses all the activities God entrusts to Jeremiah in today's reading—digging up, pulling down, building, destroying, planting, and demolishing.

It would be biblically inaccurate to categorize Jeremiah as an "innovator," at least in the capitalist sense of the word. Our text today is not a case of God reading off ideas after a brainstorming session. Rather, Jeremiah is called to be a prophet, someone who explicitly names how our current society isn't stacking up to God's hope for the world and calls on us to change it. As kin-dom innovators, prophets not only cast visions for the future, but also compel us to grief (indeed, Jeremiah is nicknamed "The Weeping Prophet") because they know that what is coming will break the hearts of their communities.

A difficult question we must pose to our communities is "What are the things we must tear down in this season that God called us to build in the last?" This question can be a source of grief and may be overwhelming to many people in faith communities. It's scary to place yesterday's blessings on today's chopping block. Beautifully crafted liturgies, hand-sewn banners, life-saving food shelves, soul-stirring songs, and cherished translations of the Bible all hold deep meaning. They survived for as long as they did for a reason. The idea that something that is so obviously sacrosanct for one person could be tossed away by another may seem almost heretical; it may feel like death itself.

Indeed, the art of innovation is in many ways a subcategory within the art of grief. Welcoming something new requires us to say farewell and to create space. It calls us to lament.

Even within the shifting religious landscape, churches still play an essential role in public grief—namely by providing space for funerals. It's curious then that an organization can be so mature in handling grief one way, but so unpracticed in another. Most churchgoers I know have deep wisdom about how to say goodbye to a loved one, but a shallow fragility when saying goodbye to traditions of the church.

As a pastor, my goals when working with people who are grieving are to help them:

(1) Express their pain honestly to themselves, others, and God.

(2) Access resources to navigate a difficult season.

(3) Find God's joy in a forever-changed future.

The approach depends on the person. I might invite people to tell stories, write farewell letters, identify a relevant Bible story, or simply pray. But we might also explore activities that help people find hope in their future. For the homesick person, we'll try mapping out parks and grocery stores near the new home. For the recent widower, we'll create a home where his spouse is honored while still being functional for the new life he must build.

What would it look like for a congregation to mourn this way? What would it look like if they wrote farewell letters to their bell choir that only two people still attend? What would it look like for a congregation to tell stories about the "good old days," while accepting that we are moving on to a forever-changed future. These are the activities that we must wrestle with. There is no cure-all that will heal the pain of community members who are trapped in grief. Usually, it involves the recognition of what has passed and demonstrating that dwelling in unprocessed grief is, in fact, more uncomfortable than living into an undefined future.

If you're reading this devotional, you're probably invested in some way in the evolution of the church so that it can match the challenges of our time. You are probably facing all sorts of unprocessed grief about how the church was, how it is, and what it will no longer be. My invitation to you is to embrace that grief and prayerfully ask yourself and your community to examine what must be torn down to make way for something new. What is yet to be properly lamented? What future vision could both recognize that lament, while also inspiring us to work together to build God's kin-dom?

Questions

- What type of grief process must your community engage to honestly express their pain to themselves, others, and God?

- What type of grief process must your community engage to access resources to navigate this difficult season?

- What type of grief process must your community engage to find God's joy in the forever-changed future?

Reading

Psalm 51:15-17 (CEB)

Lord, open my lips,
    and my mouth will proclaim your praise.
You don't want sacrifices.
    If I gave an entirely burned offering,
    you wouldn't be pleased.
A broken spirit is my sacrifice, God.
    You won't despise a heart, God, that is broken and
    crushed.

Reflection

God's love is the first and most important key to innovation. Innovation without God's love at its core is, at best, hollow and, at worst, malicious. No community, no social service, no justice movement, no art, no business, and no revolution is worthwhile without God's love.

For those embarking on the path of innovation, prayer is the essential practice that grounds us in love amid the chaotic whirlwind of creation. If there are easy answers or readily available solutions, they've already been found. Starting something new requires a love that can endure friction and dead-ends. It is not enough to be dissatisfied with the status quo; we must strive for a love that envelops us when the powers and principalities strike back.

Most mornings, I find it necessary to fill a few journal pages just to figure out where my soul is hiding. After locating myself, I try to listen for what God has to say in response, then I keep going with my day.

Yet, there are also moments when words fall short of conveying what I truly feel. Sometimes, the pain of the day manifests not in the form of thoughts or arguments but as physical sensations—an ache, a tension, a slump. In these instances, I turn to a prayer that is loosely structured like the practice of somatic experiencing, an embodied trauma therapy that I've only begun to explore (and I am by no means a therapist). Each time I try this, I notice that my body has a lot more to express to God than I'd initially realized. Here are the steps I follow:

1. Begin by standing or sitting in a neutral position and take the deepest breath you've taken all day. Shift your awareness from the external world to the sensations within your body. Playing soothing music in the background can be helpful.
2. Recall a difficult situation that you are currently grappling with and pay attention to the sensations in your body without judgment.
3. While continuing to breathe deeply, try to discern the gestures or postures your body naturally leans toward. It might want to run, reach out, collapse, stretch, constrict, or expand. Move through these actions in slow motion, as if you're moving through jelly.
4. In your new posture, invite the warm light of God's love. You might say aloud or silently, "Welcome, Holy Spirit."
5. Repeat this process, observing what your body is inclined to do without judgment, while continually inviting God's love. Avoid the temptation to make it appear perfect or artificially resolve it before it's ready. Simply express whatever surfaces.

Anything that comes up during this prayer is information. If that's boredom, then that's information. It might indicate that this is simply not the right practice, but sometimes boredom is a subtle defense in response to bringing up hard things. Yawning is information. Crying is information. The subtle, peaceful alertness that incrementally brightens up the world is information. Information isn't good or bad, just a little message your body has been trying to send you. Even as you read this, you might notice that your posture is slack, or your shoulders tense. That's information.

From a faith-based perspective, it's crucial to pay attention to this information because God desires our whole selves in prayer, including the awkward, unprocessed tensions and scathing thoughts that come up. God wants it all. God doesn't just want your peace, happiness, and joy. God also wants the anger, the cynicism, the hatred, and the despair.

The psalmist shows us that a broken spirit is a perfect offering to God. After all, God can't mend a broken heart if we're hiding it away. In my experience, there is no emotion that God does not joyfully redeem and no garbage that God cannot compost.

Honesty in prayer deepens our understanding of God's love. Rediscovering and consistently revisiting our love for God equips us for when the world punches back against our innovation. In God's love, we find peace, forgiveness, and the understanding that our worth is not tied to the success or failure of our projects.

Give it all—not just to this or that project, but to God's love. This is our truest hope.

Questions

- How does grounding innovation in God's love challenge traditional views of innovation, and what practical implications does it have?

- How can embodied prayer practices enhance our spiritual connection and support innovation driven by God's love?

- What impact does embracing and expressing ourselves in prayer have on our relationship with God and our ability to find peace and inspiration in innovation?

Stories from the Journey

In this final week of reflections, we wanted to broaden our circle and include a diverse set of voices beyond our own. These stories, each written by a different author, will highlight the principles we've explored so far during our Lenten journey and dig into how the authors are putting these principles into practice in the local church.

Sunday

Diversity

by Danielle Buwon Kim

Danielle Buwon Kim (she/her) currently serves as the Associate Director of Research and Development in the North Texas Annual Conference of The United Methodist Church. Danielle is an immigrant from South Korea who spent her later childhood in Houston, Texas.

Reading

Luke 24:30-32

When he was at the table with them, he took bread, blessed and broke it, and gave it to them. Then their eyes were opened, and they recognized him, and he vanished from their sight. They said to each other, "Were not our hearts burning within us while he was talking to us on the road, while he was opening the scriptures to us?"

Reflection

There's something truly special about sharing good Asian food and doing church around the table. Growing up as a child of immigrant parents, my earliest memories of church were centered around the table. It was a safe place for Korean immigrants, like my family, to come together and be grounded in our shared identity. It became a sanctuary for Korean foreign exchange students, soothing their homesickness. For many, it provided strength to face the daunting challenges of language barriers and long working hours. Around this table, I witnessed my elders laugh and cry. Through this table, they instilled in us such pride and resilience.

However, as a "1.5 generation" Korean American immigrant—someone who arrived in the United States as a child or adolescent—I've come to realize that my immigrant experience differs from that of my parents. Inhabiting the intersection of Korean heritage and American identity, I live in a world of both and neither, a world that is both familiar and foreign. I speak both languages fluently, yet it often seems as though I'm a master of neither. I straddle both spaces, but at times, I feel like an outsider to both. My parents and I both experience racism and microaggressions, but we do so in slightly different ways that reflect the differences in how we relate to American culture.

Indeed, many immigrant families grapple with the intergenerational trauma of immigration, while their children struggle to adapt to cultural values and norms of their adopted societies. The relentless demand for code-switching takes a toll. Many of my fellow Asian American/ Pacific Islanders (AAPIs) born in the United States or adopted into American families face the challenge of being labeled "perpetual foreigners," where their American identity is denied, and their heritage is unseen.

AAPI invisibility is a painful and enduring reality we confront daily. Our history and contributions to this country rarely receive the recognition they deserve. We're alarmingly underrepresented in politics, sports, media, business leadership, education, and the church. Despite the rich Christian heritage of many Asian and Pacific Islander groups, our liturgy and worship often center around Western Christianity. Given these unique challenges, our AAPI siblings desperately need a faith community that affirms their lived experiences and validates their discipleship journeys.

Along with many like-minded friends and fellow AAPI Christians, we began to envision a faith community where we could once again gather around the table. Our dream was to extend this table to our fellow AAPIs and friends in solidarity, offering them the chance to enjoy Asian food together, challenge and heal AAPI invisibility perpetuated by the model minority myth, and reclaim our Christian faith to liberate and reconstruct a world that more closely resembles the kin-dom of God.

After countless prayers and hours of discernment, we begin a ministry we call KA:LL Community (pronounced "call"), drawing from the Filipino concept of "ka." Jonah Ballesteros, a Filipino American and one of the leaders of KA:LL Community, shared this concept with us. "Ka" comes from the Tagalog word "kapwa," which means "to share space in union with all."

Our worship service begins by gathering around a table filled with Asian food that speaks to our souls. Instead of traditional sermons, we invite storytellers from our community to share their experiences and how they've encountered God in their lives. We then engage in communal spiritual practices, like *lectio divina* or breath prayer, or participate in open discussions. Each service ends by observing Holy Communion, proclaiming that this table has always belonged to Christ, who affirms the *imago Dei* within us and within our AAPI experiences.

Our community warmly welcomes individuals who identify as "nones" or "dones," often facing significant barriers to entering a traditional church. The table has become a safe space where they find comfort and are nurtured into a deeper communion with Christ. We persist in our prayers and labor alongside God, striving for this table to remain a safe sanctuary where we encounter Christ in a fresh, new way, a place where we confess, "Were not our hearts burning within us?"

Questions

- In what new ways have you encountered Christ recently?

- How is God challenging you to step outside your comfort zone and experience Christ in new ways?

- What does it mean to create a safe sanctuary in your own life where you can feel safe and loved by God and others?

Postcolonial

by Rev. Tweedy Evelene Sombrero Navarrete

Rev. Tweedy Evelene Sombrero Navarrete (she/her) serves as the director of Native American Ministries at Fort Yuma and Phoenix Native American Ministries. She is Diné (Navajo) and an ordained elder in the Desert Southwest Conference of The United Methodist Church.

Reading

2 Corinthians 4:8-9, 16-18

We are afflicted in every way but not crushed, perplexed but not driven to despair, persecuted but not forsaken, struck down but not destroyed.

So we do not lose heart. Even though our outer nature is wasting away, our inner nature is being renewed day by day. For our slight, momentary affliction is producing for us an eternal weight of glory beyond all measure, because we look not at what can be seen but at what cannot be seen, for what can be seen is temporary, but what cannot be seen is eternal.

Reflection

The day I uncovered the truth about my parents' past, their painful journey through boarding schools, and my identity as a child of survivors, a whirlwind of emotions engulfed me. I was sad, heartbroken, and angry. My heart ached with sorrow for the abuse my parents had to endure, and thoughts of how my own life could have been better. I can never fully fathom what my parents went through, the violence and pain they must have suffered, but I can make the commitment that this violence stops with me. It will not be carried on to my daughters' generation.

I often wonder how much shame Native people carry and what it will take to help unpack that shame and hurt. What will it take for Native people to discover that it is not their fault that this has happened. There is generational pain and hurt to work through.

Native people have survived immense atrocities throughout history, drawing strength from their spirituality and humor. The cycle of abuse they endured can end with us; we can address and halt this intergenerational suffering. It is not an easy task, but it can be done. Here are three important steps that we must take to achieve that goal:

1. **Acknowledgment:** We must acknowledge the painful truth of our history.
2. **Embrace Love and Grace:** There is no need to hide behind shame. We have love and grace to free us and guide us.
3. **Time and Forgiveness:** Healing will take time, perhaps years. It's important to recognize this and begin navigating the complex journey of forgiveness to work through it all.

Thanks be to the Creator, who walks with us through every phase of this journey. May our lives bear witness to the strength of our ancestors and serve as a testament to the power of healing. Amen.

Questions

- How can you be a resource to people as they work through their trauma?
- How do you show God's love and grace to someone who has experienced pain from people in the church?

Contextual

by Jonah Overton

Rev. Jonah P. Overton (they/them) is a community organizer, church planter, and the lead pastor of Zao MKE Church in Milwaukee, Wisconsin.

Reading

Mark 2:23-28 (CEB)

Jesus went through the wheat fields on the Sabbath. As the disciples made their way, they were picking the heads of wheat. The Pharisees said to Jesus, "Look! Why are they breaking the Sabbath law?"

He said to them, "Haven't you ever read what David did when he was in need, when he and those with him were hungry? During the time when Abiathar was high priest, David went into God's house and ate the bread of the presence, which only the priests were allowed to eat. He also gave bread to those who were with him." Then he said, "The Sabbath was created for humans; humans weren't created for the Sabbath. This is why the Human One is Lord even over the Sabbath."

Reflection

When Zao MKE Church first began gathering in a traditional church building, many members of our majority queer and trans community were uneasy about the transition. We originally started meeting in my living room. When we outgrew that, we moved to a local music venue on Sunday mornings where the floors were sticky from booze, and an herbal scent lingered in the air. We all admitted that this may not be the most glamorous location, but it offered a kind of safety to those of us who had suffered spiritual and other traumas within the walls of a conventional church building.

Eventually, the time came when we outgrew the music venue, and we were presented with the opportunity to become the primary residents of a gorgeous, historic, traditional church building right in the heart of our ministry area. Unanimously, our leadership decided to accept, feeling a call to infuse this space with a fresh, radically just and inclusive spirit. However, it wasn't long before a recurring, somewhat uneasy, joke began to surface among our community members: "I'll be struck by lightning as soon as I step foot in that building."

Many of our community members grew up in ultra-conservative religious environments governed by all kinds of rules, both spoken and unspoken. These rules dictated how we should behave in church—be quiet, don't fidget, pay attention, don't ask questions, don't laugh, giggle, dance, or hum. On and on and on they went. These rules seem innocuous on the surface, but collectively they created a culture about how to hold one's body in rigid compliance. This was particularly true for those who were already challenging (or longing to challenge) far weightier rules concerning their identity, gender, purity, and more. For queer, trans, neurodivergent, and disabled kids growing up in these churches, it felt like their very existence was an affront to God's rules.

Zao MKE Church stands as an experiment, challenging the norm by placing these rule-breakers and outcasts in charge of things. What happens when the people most marginalized by traditional church spaces are the ones leading church services? One inevitable outcome is that the rules themselves must evolve, along with the culture of unquestioning compliance.

At Zao, very few church norms go unexamined. No one needs permission before walking up to the microphone barefoot in the summer. Queer people easily and openly show affection for their partners in our space. A newcomer's hesitant apology for an accidental curse word is often met with the winking reassurance of, "No one gives a shit about that kind of thing here."

To some, this rule-breaking might seem crass or disrespectful, but at Zao, it fosters a sense of safety and freedom. During a recent small-group discussion, a community shared delight in doing things at Zao that would have gotten them in trouble in their childhood church.

"Like what?" I asked.

"Oh, everything," they replied. "Leaving in the middle of the service to go to the bathroom. Doodling or drawing. Not wearing a dress . . ."

"Or wearing a dress!" interjected another, gender-nonconforming community member.

The conversation quickly spiraled into a joyful exploration of how Zao allows people to feel free, seen, and a little rebellious by transgressing the rules of their past.

A major theme emerged: freedom of the body. Individuals reveled in wearing crop tops, taking up space, and responding to their bodily needs. One person told a story about the severe consequences they would face if they ever fell asleep during church in their youth. Yet, during a recent sermon, when they began to feel sleepy, they made a conscious choice to move to one of our comfiest couches and take a nap, confident that everyone at Zao valued responding to their body's needs.

Scripture repeatedly shows that Jesus was willing to violate religious laws and norms to meet the needs of those around him. The explanation we read in Mark 2 is quite simple: rules are made for people, not people for rules.

This teaching might unsettle many in traditional church spaces, as rules often symbolize respect and reverence. However, an excess of rules, especially those governing our bodies, can conceal deeper cultural norms that marginalize and harm people. These norms alienate us from our own physical needs, make us hyper-vigilant of not saying the wrong thing, and prioritize pleasing authority over feeling whole and seen.

Wearing a crop top to church might seem insignificant, but what if it becomes the small transgression that emboldens someone to hold their partner's hand during the service or to ask a question about a potentially harmful teaching? What if challenging norms serves as a reminder that our rules, spoken and unspoken, should serve our community, rather than the other way around?

To this day, no one at Zao has been struck by lightning. Not for swearing, not for giggling during a sermon, not for a choosing a bathroom, not for disagreeing with the pastor, and certainly not for kissing their queer beloved. The fact that we can break all these rules and still be loved and celebrated in our Christian community is a testament to the idea that these rules were never truly God's in the first place.

Questions

- What rules or norms from your church background would you love to break?

- Does rule-breaking in church make you feel free? Terrified? Annoyed?

- How can rule-breaking help us build healthier, more accountable communities?

Innovation

by Juan Pablo Herrera

Juan Pablo Herrera (he/him) is a second-generation immigrant who was born and raised in Chicago. Currently, Juan Pablo is earning a Master of Arts in Public Ministry at Garrett-Evangelical Theological Seminary and is the pastor of Urban Village Church's Wicker Park site.

Reading

Isaiah 43:15-19

I am the LORD, your Holy One,
    the Creator of Israel, your King.
Thus says the LORD,
    who makes a way in the sea,
    a path in the mighty waters,
who brings out chariot and horse,
    army and warrior;
They lie down; they cannot rise;
    they are extinguished, quenched like a wick:
Do not remember the former things
    or consider the things of old.
I am about to do a new thing;
    now it springs forth; do you not perceive it?
I will make a way in the wilderness
    and rivers in the desert.

Reflection

Six years ago, the first time I walked into an LGBTQ-inclusive church, I was immediately struck by a sense of belonging that I'd yearned for, yet never fully experienced before. At that moment, I felt as though I was standing on holy ground. It marked a pivotal awakening, a realization of a sacred space where I could embrace my true self and where my experiences were not just acknowledged, but reflected, respected, and valued.

For years, I wrestled with my identity, unsure of my place both within the church and within myself. But, that day, in that inclusive space, I had a profound revelation—God had been with me all along, through every twist and turn, every moment of doubt and affirmation. This experience not only transformed me as an individual but reshaped my role as a spiritual guide.

The concept of *lo cotidiano*, as articulated by Latino/a theologians, resonates deeply with me. This principle of ministry "in the everyday" emphasizes that knowing and understanding God originates in the lived experiences of people. In the context of the LGBTQ community in Chicago, these experiences have been marked by the dualities of life—the struggles of marginalization and the joys of celebration, the sting of injustice and the comfort of profound grace. Today, I am privileged to pastor this diverse, inclusive church that thrives on these very principles. Every day, I am touched by the unique stories of faith, struggle, resilience, and triumph that fill our sanctuary.

However, what truly surprises me is the spirit of the young adults. Their vibrant energy, fearless questioning, and commitment to effect change amazes me. They are not merely churchgoers; they are the innovative spiritual leaders of our community today. And at the heart of their drive is the principle of *lo cotidiano* that drives them.

These young adults apply this liberative theological concept to build community. They draw from their daily experiences, the stories that define them, and the rhythms of their lives to foster connection, understanding, and love. This approach gives them the freedom to use their creativity to design their own small communities—small groups that read together, host game nights, go country dancing, create art, and more, all to connect with others beyond the church's four walls. They see themselves not just as members of our congregation but as ministers—vital contributors to our community's spiritual growth and well-being.

They initiate dialogues on social justice, organize events celebrating our diversity, and champion policies ensuring our church remains inclusive. They do not wait to be called; they take the initiative, driven by the belief that their actions, whether big or small, can make a difference. In doing so, they inspire all of us to view our everyday lives, our *lo cotidiano*, as the sacred groundwork for understanding God, serving humanity, and nurturing our spiritual selves.

Six years ago, I walked into an inclusive church that changed my life. Today, I lead that same beautifully diverse congregation that continues to change lives. I am honored to bear witness to and be a part of this vibrant dance of faith, where young adults, empowered by the concept of *lo cotidiano*, step forward as today's innovative leaders and ministers.

To me, this is the essence of our church—a place where everyone, regardless of their age, race, sexuality, or life story, is seen, heard, valued, and empowered. Here, we understand God through our shared and individual experiences, through the rhythm of our everyday lives. Together, we are shaping a faith community that reflects the inclusive love of God—a testament to the transformative power of love, understanding, and authenticity.

Questions

- How does the principle of lo cotidiano challenge or reshape traditional concepts of ministry and spiritual leadership, especially in the context of LGBTQ inclusion in the church?

- Reflecting on the role of young adults in the church, how does their understanding and application of lo cotidiano influence their approach to building community and initiating change?

- Considering your own journey, in what ways has your personal experience and story impacted your vision for the future of the church and its members?

Thursday

Equity

by Tasha Mitchell

Tasha Mitchell (she/her) is currently a Ph.D. student in the Pastoral Theology, Personality and Culture program at Garrett-Evangelical Seminary and a counselor at Relational Insight, Inc. She completed her M. Div. at Vanderbilt Divinity School with a triple concentration in Religion and Economic Justice, Spirituality and Social Activism, and Black Religion and Culture Studies.

Readings

2 Corinthians 9:6-9

The point is this: the one who sows sparingly will also reap sparingly, and the one who sows bountifully will also reap bountifully. Each of you must give as you have made up your mind, not regretfully or under compulsion, for God loves a cheerful giver. And God is able to provide you with every blessing in abundance, so that by always having enough of everything, you may share abundantly in every good work. As it is written,

> "He scatters abroad; he gives to the poor;
>> his righteousness endures
>> forever."

Reflection

I can vividly recall the first time greed entered my young life. I couldn't have been more than six or seven years old and I was spending the day with one of my childhood BFFs from our apartment complex, whom we'll call "Mikey" to protect his privacy. Mikey and I were thick as thieves, playing outside or at each other's houses and generally exploring the world together as kids do. I lived with my single father and two sisters, while Mikey lived with his grandmother. Although I can't quite remember the backstory that led to Mikey's living situation, I believe it's a crucial detail in this story. We were two underprivileged kids navigating life under less-than-ideal circumstances, but more importantly, we were friends.

On this particular afternoon, I found Mikey indulging in a pack of fruit snacks while sitting on the steps in front of his apartment building. Any parent or anyone familiar with children knows that fruit snacks are pretty much gummy gold for a kid. I wanted to delight in this treasure with him. When Mikey realized this, he excitedly jumped up and ran inside, returning with two more packs of fruit snacks—one for himself and one for me. We sat side by side, enjoying our bounty, but as I savored mine, I noticed Mikey quickly finishing his second pack. Then, it happened—he told me that I should share my remaining fruit snacks with him. As you can imagine, a heated argument ensued, leading to both of us tattling on each other to our respective caregivers. The altercation ended with Mikey's grandmother giving him a third pack of gummy gold for his troubles, while I stewed in my indignation for the remainder of the day.

At some point, Mikey moved away, and our friendship dissolved. This was the early nineties, a time before widespread internet, text messaging, or direct messages. I have no idea where life took Mikey, but I can say that the impact of his actions remains with me today. In hindsight, that incident probably shaped my theology, politics, and worldview more than I initially realized. Even as a child, I keenly felt the injustice and greed in Mikey's request. It felt wrong and unfair. How dare he eat two whole fruit snack packs and then have the audacity to demand I share what little he had given me? But when I look at our world today, I stop and quickly say, "Oh, yes, this tracks."

We inhabit a world fraught with greedy, sinful systems that breed unfathomable inequity, and this inequity is palpable in our lived experience. It fosters a myth of scarcity that compels us to prioritize ourselves above all else. Instead of embracing genuine cooperation, contentment, and charity, we've been persuaded by the empire to pursue competitive gain at the expense of collective well-being. It's a deceitful trap, one that fuels conflicts among us rather than uniting us to dismantle the oppressive systems under which we all suffer. We're conditioned to believe our desires and wants matter most, leading us to overlook and even marginalize others, replicating the injustices we've suffered ourselves.

And where does this path lead us? To a ceaseless rat race where everyone competes to consume more, even at the cost of others, just as Mikey did when we were kids. It discourages us from fully embodying the cheerful giver that Paul speaks about in his letter to the Corinthians and encourages us to mask our underlying self-centeredness with a façade of fake benevolence.

We must resist the temptation to mirror the powerful entities that govern our world. Instead, we must challenge ourselves to fulfill the greatest commandment, as articulated by Jesus: to love God, and to love others as we love ourselves. Perhaps that means the next time you grab two packs of fruit snacks for yourself, you also pick up two for your unhoused neighbor as well. Perhaps it starts with that, and then grows into so much more.

Questions

- Reflect on the call to resist mirroring the self-centered behaviors of powerful entities and instead prioritize loving God and others. What steps can you take to embody this principle in your daily life?

- What changes or shifts in perspective do you think are necessary for individuals and society as a whole to move away from a mindset of scarcity and greed toward one of cooperation and collective well-being?

- Are there specific actions or practices you can commit to that align with the idea of becoming a "cheerful giver," as mentioned in the reading today?

Good Friday

by Candace Lewis

Reading

Luke 23:34

Then Jesus said, "Father, forgive them, for they do not know what they are doing." And they cast lots to divide his clothing.

Reflection

In this first word, we encounter Jesus,
Betrayed, denied, abandoned, arrested, accused, tried, examined
Condemned, bruised, whipped, ridiculed, mocked, punished
Rejected, cursed, sentenced, flogged, taunted, weakened
Followed, mourned, wailed, crucified, nailed, bloodied, suffered
Executed, beloved, resolved, focused, purposed, pained
Human, divine, innocent, dying
Yet still speaking. . . .
He uttered, the first word,
"Father forgive them, for they do not know what they are doing."

Jesus first calls his Father, acknowledging the relationship with God that has been with him from the beginning and remains with him even now, even in his darkest hours. Father. And there are so many things Jesus could have asked his Father for at a time like this . . .

Father, save
Father, deliver
Father, heal
Father, change
Father, forgive. . . .

Father forgive them, but who is them?

"For they, do not know what they are doing"—they acted in ignorance.

Three questions emerge for me, as we wrestle with Jesus' first word shared from the cross:

Do we really believe today that people murder others out of ignorance?

I'm not going to retraumatize us by walking through the litany of names, the men, women, and children who have been murdered by the actions of the police. I won't be listing all those who were murdered through domestic violence, femicide, gun violence, or school shootings. Ignorance?

Do we believe that people who murder others do not know what they are doing?

All it takes is reading or hearing about a school shooter's manifesto to know that they had some idea of what the were doing. Ignorance?

Do we believe today that people who murder others should be forgiven for their actions?

Why would Jesus utter these words, these challenging, difficult words, as the first of seven sayings from the cross? Why would he say this as he prepares to take his final breath?

I think the weight of unforgiveness is too heavy to bear.

Questions

- How do the words, "Father forgive them, for they do not know what they are doing," challenge our understanding of forgiveness?

- How does this reflection challenge our society's approach to addressing acts of violence, particularly in cases where the perpetrators may have acted with some level of awareness?

Saturday

Holy Saturday

by Matt Temple

Reading

Genesis 21:15-19, 33-34

When the water in the skin was gone, she cast the child under one of the bushes. Then she went and sat down opposite him a good way off, about the distance of a bowshot, for she said, "Do not let me look on the death of the child." And as she sat opposite him, she lifted up her voice and wept. And God heard the voice of the boy, and the angel of God called to Hagar from heaven and said to her, "What troubles you, Hagar? Do not be afraid, for God has heard the voice of the boy where he is. Come, lift up the boy and hold him fast with your hand, for I will make a great nation of him." Then God opened her eyes, and she saw a well of water. She went and filled the skin with water and gave the boy a drink. Abraham planted a tamarisk tree in Beer-sheba, and called there on the name of the LORD, the Everlasting God. And Abraham resided as an alien for many days in the land of the Philistines.

Reflection

I've made some difficult phone calls in my life, but this particular one ranks among the toughest. When I first joined my evangelical charismatic denomination, I was a wide-eyed, enthusiastic fifteen-year-old, eager to dedicate my life to serving the church. Sixteen years later as an ordained pastor, I found myself making a life-altering phone call that would bring all that to an end. It took me several years to come to terms with this reality, but it had become clear that my faith journey and my understanding of God's inclusive nature had diverged from the theological vision of those I had served alongside for so many years. We were now growing in different directions. I harbored no illusions. I knew that as soon as I made this call, many of the people I considered friends would no longer be interested in continuing our friendship. I knew that the narrative about me might not be flattering, despite my years of dedicated service. Nevertheless, I knew it was the right thing to do.

When you've invested nearly two decades in one organization and decide to walk away, you hear a lot of doors slam shut behind you. You're left with little clarity about which, if any, doors will open in the future. I'm so grateful that, after several months of uncertainty and wandering, I stumbled upon the people called United Methodist, where I found a new home. However, that season in between, that season of not knowing, was one of the hardest seasons I've ever faced.

In Genesis 21, we find Abraham in a similar place of loss and uncertainty. He had risked everything, believing in God's promise—a promise centered on people and land. Yet, in Genesis 21, Abraham is reminded that he still lacks these two crucial elements. Prior to verses 33 and 34, Abraham had sent away his firstborn son, gotten in a squabble with the ruler of the Philistines over the use of some wells, and was reminded yet again that he was an undocumented immigrant in a land that was not his own. The future of his people and the promise from God seemed to hang in the balance. In this moment, in this place called Beer-sheba, Abraham calls out to El Olam, the Everlasting God.

I ran across this text again during my own season of waiting. I discovered that the Hebrew word *olam* literally means "vanishing point." Picture yourself standing on a beach, watching the sunset. There's a moment when the sun seems to disappear, but even though it has vanishes from our sight, we know it's still there, setting the sky ablaze with breathtaking brilliance. The vanishing point is that moment beyond our grasp, beyond our control, where genuine faith is ignited.

This story isn't the first or the last time that the God who is faithful beyond the vanishing point shows up. Just a bit earlier in the chapter, Hagar experiences the same thing. In a scene similar to Abraham's near sacrifice of Isaac, Hagar sets her son, Ishmael, down and walks away, not wanting to see him die. In that moment, the God who remains faithful beyond life's vanishing points shows up, providing water and a promise of a future. Several years later, Jacob meets God in the very same place. In the midst of a famine, where the survival of God's people once again hangs in the balance, he cries out to God, and the God who remains faithful beyond life's vanishing points meets him, directing him to go to Egypt. God promises to save God's people. Jacob, like the others, is reminded that there's a promise for the future. In their own way, Abraham, Hagar, and Jacob all encounter this God who is faithful beyond the vanishing points of life when their uncertain future threatens to swallow their hope.

On this Holy Saturday, let us cling to the promise that even in the darkest moments, when hope seems elusive, El Olam is present. The resurrection of Jesus on Easter Sunday proclaims God's power to breathe life into the most desolate places, to resurrect dreams, and ignite the flame of hope within us. In the waiting, we discover that our longings are not in vain; rather, they are a catalyst for a profound encounter with the living God. As we gaze into the unknown, may we lift our eyes to the sky to see it lit with the evidence that even though we don't know what lies beyond the vanishing point, we can rest assured that God will be faithful!

Questions

- In what ways can Hagar's story be seen as a narrative of resilience and empowerment? How might her experience of encountering God in the wilderness be a source of inspiration for individuals facing challenges today?

- Hagar's encounter with the divine challenges conventional notions of who can experience God's presence. How might her story encourage a more inclusive and diverse understanding of spirituality and religious experiences?

- Seasons of waiting, uncertainty, and not knowing are difficult. Have you ever experienced a period of waiting or uncertainty in your life? How did it feel and how did that experience form you?

Sunday

Easter Sunday

by Rachel Gilmore

Reading

John 20:1-18

Early on the first day of the week, while it was still dark, Mary Magdalene came to the tomb and saw that the stone had been removed from the tomb. So she ran and went to Simon Peter and the other disciple, the one whom Jesus loved, and said to them, "They have taken the Lord out of the tomb, and we do not know where they have laid him." Then Peter and the other disciple set out and went toward the tomb. The two were running together, but the other disciple outran Peter and reached the tomb first. He bent down to look in and saw the linen wrappings lying there, but he did not go in. Then Simon Peter came, following him, and went into the tomb. He saw the linen wrappings lying there, and the cloth that had been on Jesus' head, not lying with the linen wrappings but rolled up in a place by itself. Then the other disciple, who reached the tomb first, also went in, and he saw and believed; for as yet they did not understand the scripture, that he must rise from the dead. Then the disciples returned to their homes.

But Mary stood weeping outside the tomb. As she wept, she bent over to look into the tomb; and she saw two angels in white, sitting where the body of Jesus had been lying, one at the head and the other at the feet. They said to her, "Woman, why are you weeping?" She said to them, "They have taken away my Lord, and I do not know where they have laid him." When she had said this, she turned around and saw Jesus standing there, but she did not know that it was Jesus. Jesus said to her, "Woman, why are you weeping? Whom are you looking for?" Supposing him to be the gardener, she said to him, "Sir, if you have carried him away, tell me where you have laid him, and I will take him away." Jesus said to her, "Mary!" She turned and said to him in Hebrew,[b] "Rabbouni!" (which means Teacher). Jesus said to her, "Do not hold on to me, because I have not yet ascended to the Father. But go to my brothers and say to them, 'I am ascending to my Father and your Father, to my God and your God.'" Mary Magdalene went and announced to the disciples, "I have seen the Lord"; and she told them that he had said these things to her.

Reflection

Christ is risen! He has risen indeed! I love John's account of the Resurrection. It reminds us of the gifts we all bring to our faith journey and how deeply we need one another as we walk this path together.

Let's look more closely at the lives of the people in this remarkable story. First, there's Mary Magdalene. Jesus had cast demons out from her, and it's suggested she was a wealthy widow who had the means to follow Jesus on his travels. She stood unwaveringly at the foot of the cross and, when Jesus breathed his last, her grief was all-consuming. As soon as the Sabbath ended, she hurried to the tomb, driven by her desire to be near his body and be close to Jesus in her sorrow. Upon discovering the stone rolled away, she raced to find John and Peter.

John might have been one of the "Sons of Thunder" but, in scripture, we see him portrayed as a loyal and loving follower of Christ. He was a disciple of John the Baptist before joining up with Jesus. He is the one who reclines against Jesus during the Last Supper. John's devotion is evident. He is the only disciple standing close at Jesus' crucifixion, and he is given the responsibility to care for Jesus' mother, Mary. Despite his swiftness in reaching the tomb ahead of Peter, he didn't immediately go inside. It was only later, after following Peter inside, that he saw and believed, yet he kept his revelation to himself. John would go on to be the sole disciple to die a natural death in old age, tirelessly telling the story of Christ for decades to come.

Peter, known for his boldness and bluntness, wasted no time entering the tomb upon his arrival. Though he couldn't grasp the significance of what he saw, he plunged forward. Throughout scripture, Peter says what others dared not speak, such as when he acknowledges Jesus as the

Son of God. He was unafraid to go where others wouldn't, even step-ping out of a boat to walk on water toward Jesus. Peter had just faced the shame of publicly denying Christ and now grappled with confusion and uncertainty about his relationship with God.

In John's account of Easter morning, we are reminded that without Mary, Peter, and John, these events might have unfolded differently. Their unique strengths and characteristics complemented one another. Without Mary, Peter and John would not have known to run to the tomb. Without Peter's boldness, John might not have ventured inside, and without John, we might not have an account of someone believing in the Easter event without directly encountering the risen Christ.

The undeniable truth is that we need one another. We cannot fol-low Christ in isolation; we were created for community, mirroring the trinitarian communal existence of God for all of eternity. We need one another. We rely on one another's gifts as we continue to embrace and reflect the good news of Easter morning.

Sometimes we are like Mary, consumed by our losses and the changes in our lives, making it challenging to recognize the Resurrec-tion life right in front of us. Yet our desire to be near Jesus and our invitation to others leads them to profound encounters with God.

Sometimes we are like Peter, brimming with energy and opinions, eager to understand so we can build something long-lasting. How-ever, peer pressure and a desire to be on the "winning" side can lead to betraying what we hold dear, only to later dedicate our lives to those very ideals.

Sometimes we are like John—nurturing, loving, loyal, and inquisi-tive. We possess a deep curiosity for God and unwavering belief, yet we leave the tomb, like John, still pondering and not yet ready to proclaim our insights.

As Mary left the tomb, she encounters Jesus, but she doesn't know it. Maybe it was the intensity of her grief that blinded her to the truth of resurrected life. Maybe Jesus' outer form looked different after the Resurrection. Perhaps he looked completely transformed and she could not see him for who he was. Yet, when Jesus called her name, she immediately recognized him and she ran to share the good news of his Resurrection with her community.

We, as the church, are a continuation of the Incarnation. We are the body of Christ in the world. Change and uncertainty may grip us; we may fear for the church's future. But take heart! Christ has overcome death and risen from the grave. Christ has transformed us and given us life. The church may change; it may look different, and those who have followed the church for years may not recognize it in its resurrected form at first, but as when Jesus called Mary by her name and she immediately recognized him, so will the people of God recognize the church when it shares the good news of Resurrection with the world.

This Easter, let us nurture the relationships within our communities and call out one another's names as we journey together into this new chapter of our shared faith. Christ is risen! He is risen indeed! Thanks be to God!

Questions

- Who are you in the Easter story?

- If you feel alone or isolated in your faith, who can you reach out to and find a sense of belonging or community?

- If the church is a continuation of the incarnation and we are called to bring God's love and hope wherever we go, then what is your role in that process? How are you helping? Who are you serving? Where are you sharing love and hope?